Careers in Focus

GEOLOGY

Ferguson's

An Infobase Learning Company

Careers in Focus: Geology

Copyright © 2012 by Infobase Learning

Ferguson's
An imprint of Infobase Learning
132 West 31st Street
New York NY 10001

Library of Congress Cataloging-in-Publication Data

Careers in focus. Geology. — 1st ed.
    p. cm.
    Includes bibliographical references and index.
    ISBN-13: 978-0-8160-8042-7 (hardcover : alk. paper)
    ISBN-10: 0-8160-8042-9 (hardcover : alk. paper)   1. Geology—Vocational guidance—Juvenile literature.   I. Ferguson Publishing.   II. Title: Geology.
    QE34.C38 2011
    550.23—dc23

                                                              2011022445

Ferguson's books are available at special discounts when purchased in bulk quantities for businesses, associations, institutions, or sales promotions. Please call our Special Sales Department in New York at (212) 967-8800 or (800) 322-8755.

You can find Ferguson's on the World Wide Web at
http://www.infobaselearning.com

Text design by David Strelecky
Composition by Newgen North America
Cover printed by Yurchak Printing, Landisville, Pa.
Book printed and bound by Yurchak Printing, Landisville, Pa.
Date printed: November 2011
Printed in the United States of America

10 9 8 7 6 5 4 3 2 1

This book is printed on acid-free paper.

All links and Web addresses were checked and verified to be correct at the time of publication. Because of the dynamic nature of the Web, some addresses and links may have changed since publication and may no longer be valid.

Table of Contents

Introduction

Geology is the science of the earth's history, composition, and structure. It is divided into two main branches: physical geology and historical geology.

Physical geology investigates the composition and structure of rocks and the forces that bring about change in the earth's crust. This branch includes *economic geology*, the study of the exploration of natural resources; *engineering geology*, the study of the earth's crust and resulting geologic phenomena (such as earthquakes and erosion) with human-made structures; *geochemistry*, the analysis of the chemical composition of the earth's crust; *geomorphology*, the description and study of landforms; *geophysics*, the study of matter and energy and how they interact; *mineralogy*, the study of the chemical and physical properties of minerals; *petrology*, the study of the origin, occurrence, structure, and history of rocks; *sedimentology*, the study of sediments and the processes (such as wind and water) that cause them to be displaced; *seismology*, the study of earthquake shocks and their effects; and *structural geology*, the investigation of stresses and strains in the earth's crust and the deformations they produce.

Historical geology is the second branch of geology. It examines rocks for evidence of conditions on the earth's surface millions of years ago. It also traces the rise of plant and animal life as revealed by fossils. This branch includes *geochronology*, the study of time in relation to the history of the earth; *geologic mapping*, the superimposing of historical geologic data on existing topographic maps; *paleontology*, the study of fossils; *paleogeography*, the study of the locations of ancient land masses; and *stratigraphy*, the classification of rock sequences.

Employment settings vary greatly for geoscientists. Some work in offices, classrooms, and in laboratories. Many conduct extensive research in the field in a variety of physical environments and weather conditions.

Geologists and other geoscience professionals are employed by local, state, and federal agencies (such as the U.S. Geological Survey, Bureau of Reclamation, National Oceanic and Atmospheric Administration, U.S. Fish & Wildlife Service, National Geodetic Survey, Bureau of Land Management, Army Corps of Engineers, National Science Foundation, National Aeronautics and Space Administration, Environmental Protection Agency, National Geospatial-Intelligence

Agency, and National Park Service), colleges and universities, museums, nonprofit organizations, and in private industry (by energy companies, consulting firms, engineering services firms, law firms, construction companies, utility companies, and any other organization that requires geological expertise).

Employment for geoscientists will grow faster than the average for all occupations through 2018, according to the U.S. Department of Labor (DOL). The DOL says that "the need for energy, environmental protection, and responsible land and water management will spur employment demand." Growth will also occur as a result of an increase in construction projects that are geared towards repairing our nation's infrastructure, such as highways and bridges. The best jobs will go to bilingual geoscientists with master's degrees who are willing to work abroad. Employment is expected to be best in the private sector since many government agencies, such as the U.S. Geological Survey, are cutting budgets and contracting out positions to consulting firms in the private sector.

Each article in *Careers in Focus: Geology* discusses a particular geological career in detail. Many of the articles in the book appear in Ferguson's *Encyclopedia of Careers and Vocational Guidance*, but have been updated and revised with the latest information from the U.S. Department of Labor and other sources.

The **Quick Facts** section provides a brief summary of the career including recommended school subjects, personal skills, work environment, minimum educational requirements, salary ranges, certification or licensing requirements, and employment outlook. This section also provides acronyms and identification numbers for the following government classification indexes: the Dictionary of Occupational Titles (DOT), the Guide for Occupational Exploration (GOE), the National Occupational Classification (NOC) Index, and the Occupational Information Network (O*NET)-Standard Occupational Classification System (SOC) index. The DOT, GOE, and O*NET-SOC indexes have been created by the U.S. government; the NOC index is Canada's career classification system. Readers can use the identification numbers listed in the Quick Facts section to access further information about a career. Print editions of the DOT (*Dictionary of Occupational Titles*. Indianapolis, Ind.: JIST Works, 1991) and GOE (*Guide for Occupational Exploration*. Indianapolis, Ind.: JIST Works, 2001) are available at libraries. Electronic versions of the DOT (http://www.oalj.dol.gov/libdot.htm), NOC (http://www5 .hrsdc.gc.ca/NOC), and O*NET-SOC (http://www.onetonline.org) are available on the Internet. When no DOT, GOE, NOC, or O*NET-SOC numbers are listed, this means that the U.S. Department of Labor or Human Resources and Skills Development Canada have not created a numerical designation for this career. In this instance, you will see the acronym "N/A," or not available.

The **Overview** section is a brief introductory description of the duties and responsibilities involved in this career. Oftentimes, a career may have a variety of job titles. When this is the case, alternative career titles are presented. Employment statistics are also provided, when available. The **History** section describes the history of the particular job as it relates to the overall development of its industry or field. The **Job** describes the primary and secondary duties of the job. **Requirements** discusses high school and postsecondary education and training requirements, any certification or licensing that is necessary, and other personal requirements for success in the job. **Exploring** offers suggestions on how to gain experience in or knowledge of the particular job before making a firm educational and financial commitment. The focus is on what can be done while still in high school (or in the early years of college) to gain a better understanding of the job. The **Employers** section gives an overview of typical places of employment for the job. **Starting Out** discusses the best ways to land that first job, be it through the college career services office, newspaper ads, Internet employment sites, or personal contact. The **Advancement** section describes what kind of career path to expect from the job and how to get there. **Earnings** lists salary ranges and describes the typical fringe benefits. The **Work Environment** section describes the typical surroundings and conditions of employment—whether indoors or outdoors, noisy or quiet, social or independent. Also discussed are typical hours worked, any seasonal fluctuations, and the stresses and strains of the job. The **Outlook** section summarizes the job in terms of the general economy and industry projections. For the most part, Outlook information is obtained from the U.S. Bureau of Labor Statistics and is supplemented by information gathered from professional associations. Job growth terms follow those used in the *Occupational Outlook Handbook*. Growth described as "much faster than the average" means an increase of 20 percent or more. Growth described as "faster than the average" means an increase of 14 to 19 percent. Growth described as "about as fast as the average" means an increase of 7 to 13 percent. Growth described as "more slowly than the average" means an increase of 3 to 6 percent. "Little or no change" means a decrease of 2 percent to an increase of 2 percent. "Decline" means a decrease of 3 percent or more. Each article ends with **For More Information**, which lists organizations that provide information on training, education, internships, scholarships, and job placement.

Careers in Focus: Geology also includes photographs, informative sidebars, and interviews with professionals in the field.

College Professors, Geology

QUICK FACTS

School Subjects
Earth science
Speech

Personal Skills
Communication/ideas
Helping/teaching

Work Environment
Indoors and outdoors
One location with some
travel

Minimum Education Level
Master's degree

Salary Range
$43,980 to $82,840 to
$148,970+

Certification or Licensing
Voluntary

Outlook
Faster than the average

DOT
090

GOE
12.03.02

NOC
4121

O*NET-SOC
25-1051.00

OVERVIEW

College geology professors instruct undergraduate and graduate students about geology and related subjects at colleges and universities. They lecture classes, supervise labs, and create and grade examinations. They also conduct field research, write for publication, and aid in administration. Approximately 9,900 postsecondary atmospheric, earth, marine, and space sciences teachers are employed in the United States.

HISTORY

The concept of colleges and universities goes back many centuries. These institutions evolved slowly from monastery schools, which trained a select few for certain professions, notably theology. The terms *college* and *university* have become virtually interchangeable in America outside the walls of academia, although originally they designated two very different kinds of institutions.

Two of the most notable early European universities were the University of Bologna in Italy and the University of Paris. The University of Bologna is thought to have been established in the 12th century, and the University of Paris was chartered in 1201. These universities were considered to be models after which other European universities were patterned. Oxford University in England was probably established during the 12th century. Oxford served as a model for early American colleges and universities and today is still considered one of the world's leading institutions.

A geology professor (left) instructs his physical geology class during a field study. *(Will Powers, AP Photo)*

Harvard, the first U.S. college, was established in 1636. Its stated purpose was to train men for the ministry. All of the early colleges were established for religious training. With the growth of state-supported institutions in the early 18th century, the process of freeing the curriculum from ties with the church began. The University of Virginia established the first liberal arts curriculum in 1825, and these innovations were later adopted by many other colleges and universities.

Although the original colleges in the United States were patterned after Oxford University, they later came under the influence of German universities. During the 19th century, more than 9,000 Americans went to Germany to study. The emphasis in German universities was on the scientific method. Most of the people who had studied in Germany returned to the United States to teach in universities, bringing this objective, factual approach to education, the sciences (including chemistry, biology, earth science, and mathematics), and other fields of learning.

THE JOB

College and university faculty members teach geology and other earth science-related subjects at junior colleges or at four-year colleges and universities. At four-year institutions, most faculty members are *assistant professors, associate professors*, or *full professors*. These three types of professorships differ in regards to status, job responsibilities, and salary. Assistant professors are new faculty members who are working to get tenure (status as a permanent professor); they seek to advance to associate and then to full professorships.

College geology professors perform three main functions: teaching, service, and research. Their most important responsibility is to teach students. Their role within the department will determine the level of courses they teach and the number of courses per semester. Most professors work with students at all levels, from college freshmen to graduate students. They may teach several classes a semester or only a few a year. Though professors may spend only 12 to 16 hours a week in the actual classroom, they spend many hours preparing lesson plans, grading assignments and exams, and preparing grade reports. They also schedule office or computer laboratory hours during the week to be available to students outside of regular classes, and they meet with students individually throughout the semester. Many professors also work in the field as practicing geologists.

In the classroom, professors lecture, lead discussions, administer exams, and assign textbook reading and other research. In some courses, they rely heavily on laboratories to transmit course material. In addition to teaching classes, professors also administer exams and assign textbook reading and other research.

An important part of teaching is advising students. Not all geology professors serve as advisers, but those who do must set aside large blocks of time to guide students through the program. College professors who serve as advisers may have any number of students assigned to them, from fewer than 10 to more than 100, depending on the administrative policies of the college. Their responsibilities may involve looking over a planned program of studies to make sure the students meet requirements for graduation, or they may have to work intensively with each student on many aspects of college life. They may also discuss the different geology specialties with students and help them identify the best career choices.

The third responsibility of geology professors is research and publication. Faculty members who are heavily involved in research programs sometimes are assigned a smaller teaching load. Publishing a significant amount of work has been the traditional standard by which assistant geology professors prove themselves worthy of becoming permanent, tenured faculty. Typically, pressure to publish is greatest for assistant professors. Pressure to publish increases again if an associate professor wishes to be considered for a promotion to full professorship. Professors in junior colleges face less pressure to publish than those in four-year institutions. College geology professors publish their research findings in various scholarly journals, such as *Geology, Geosphere*, and *Environmental & Engineering Geoscience*. They also write books based on their research or on their own knowledge and experience in the field. Most textbooks are written by college and university teachers.

All college professors provide important services to their department, college, or profession. Many college professors edit technical journals, review research and scholarship, and head committees about their field of expertise. College professors also serve on committees that determine the curriculum or make decisions about student learning.

Some faculty members eventually rise to the position of *geology department chair*, where they govern the affairs of the entire department. Department chairs, faculty, and other professional staff members are aided in their myriad duties by *graduate assistants*, who may help develop teaching materials, conduct research, give examinations, teach lower-level courses, and carry out other activities.

Some college professors may also conduct classes in an extension program. In such a program, they teach evening and weekend courses for the benefit of people who otherwise would not be able to take advantage of the institution's resources. They may travel away from the campus and meet with a group of students at another location. They may work full time for the extension division or may divide their time between on-campus and off-campus teaching.

Distance learning programs, an increasingly popular option for students, give geology professors the opportunity to use today's technologies to remain in one place while teaching students who are at a variety of locations simultaneously. The professor's duties, like those when teaching correspondence courses conducted by mail, include grading work that students send in at periodic intervals and advising students of their progress. Computers, the Internet, e-mail, and video conferencing, however, are some of the technology tools that allow professors and students to communicate in "real time" in a virtual classroom setting. Meetings may be scheduled during the same time as traditional classes or during evenings and weekends. Professors who do this work are sometimes known as *extension work, correspondence*, or *distance learning instructors*. They may teach online courses in addition to other classes or may have distance learning as their major teaching responsibility.

The *junior college instructor* has many of the same kinds of responsibilities as does the professor in a four-year college or university. Because junior colleges offer only a two-year program, they teach only undergraduates.

REQUIREMENTS

High School
Your high school's college preparatory program likely includes courses in English, science (especially earth science), foreign language, history, math, and government. In addition, you should take courses in speech to get a sense of what it will be like to lecture to a group of students. Your school's debate team can also help you develop public speaking skills, along with research skills.

Postsecondary Training
At least one advanced degree in geology or another earth science field is required to be a professor in a college or university. The master's degree is considered the minimum standard, and graduate work beyond the master's is usually desirable. If you hope to advance in academic rank above instructor, most institutions require a doctorate.

In the last year of your undergraduate program, you'll apply to graduate programs in your area of study. Standards for admission to a graduate program can be high and the competition heavy, depending on the school. Once accepted into a program, your responsibilities will be similar to those of your professors—in addition to attending seminars, you'll research, prepare articles for publication, and teach some undergraduate courses.

You may find employment in a junior college with only a master's degree. Advancement in responsibility and in salary, however, is more likely to come if you have earned a doctorate.

Certification or Licensing
There is no certification or licensing available for geology professors. Practicing geologists can obtain voluntary certification from the American Institute of Professional Geologists.

Other Requirements
You should enjoy reading, writing, and researching. Not only will you spend many years studying in school, but your whole career will be based on communicating your thoughts and ideas. People skills are important because you'll be dealing directly with students, administrators, and other faculty members on a daily basis. You should feel comfortable in a role of authority and possess self-confidence.

EXPLORING

Your high school teachers use many of the same skills as college professors, so talk to your teachers about their careers and their college experiences. You can develop your own teaching experience by volunteering at a community center, working at a day care center, or working at a summer camp (especially one that focuses on geology or another earth science). Also, spend some time on a college campus to get a sense of the environment. Write to colleges for their admissions brochures and course catalogs (or check them out online); read about the faculty members in geology departments and the courses they teach. Before visiting college campuses, make arrangements to speak to professors who teach courses that interest you. These professors may allow you to sit in on their classes and observe. Also, make appointments with college advisers and with people in the admissions and recruitment offices. If your grades are good enough, you might be able to serve as a teaching assistant during your undergraduate years, which can give you experience leading discussions and grading papers.

EMPLOYERS

Approximately 9,900 postsecondary atmospheric, earth, marine, and space sciences teachers are employed in the United States. Employment opportunities vary based on area of study and education. With a doctorate, a number of publications, and a record of good teaching, professors should find opportunities in universities all across the country. Geology professors teach in undergraduate and graduate programs. The teaching jobs at doctoral institutions are usually better paying and more prestigious. The most sought-after positions are those that offer tenure. Teachers that have only a master's degree will be limited to opportunities with junior colleges, community colleges, and some small private institutions.

STARTING OUT

You should start the process of finding a teaching position while you are in graduate school. The process includes developing a *curriculum vitae* (a detailed, academic resume), writing for publication, assisting with research, attending conferences, and gaining teaching experience and recommendations. Many students begin applying for teaching positions while finishing their graduate program. For most positions at four-year institutions, you must travel to large conferences where interviews can be arranged with representatives from the universities to which you have applied.

Because of the competition for tenure-track positions, you may have to work for a few years in temporary positions, visiting various schools as an adjunct professor. Some professional associations maintain lists of teaching opportunities in their areas. They may also make lists of applicants available to college administrators looking to fill an available position.

ADVANCEMENT

The normal pattern of advancement is from instructor to assistant professor, to associate professor, to full professor. All four academic ranks are concerned primarily with teaching and research. College faculty members who have an interest in and a talent for administration may be advanced to chair of a department or to dean of their college. A few become college or university presidents or other types of administrators.

The instructor is usually an inexperienced college teacher. He or she may hold a doctorate or may have completed all the Ph.D. requirements except for the dissertation. Most colleges look upon the rank of instructor as the period during which the college is trying out the teacher. Instructors usually are advanced to the position of assistant professors within three to four years. Assistant professors are given up to about six years to prove themselves worthy of tenure, and if they do so, they become associate professors. Some professors choose to remain at the associate level. Others strive to become full professors and receive greater status, salary, and responsibilities.

Most colleges have clearly defined promotion policies from rank to rank for faculty members, and many have written statements about the number of years in which instructors and assistant professors may remain in grade. Administrators in many colleges hope to encourage younger faculty members to increase their skills and competencies and thus to qualify for the more responsible positions of associate professor and full professor.

EARNINGS

Earnings vary by the departments professors work in, by the size of the school, by the type of school (public, private, women's only, for example), and by the level of position the professor holds.

According to the U.S. Department of Labor (DOL), in 2010, the median salary for postsecondary earth sciences teachers was $82,840, with 10 percent earning $148,970 or more and 10 percent earning $43,980 or less. Earth sciences teachers employed at junior colleges had mean annual earnings of $87,830. Those with the highest earnings tend to be senior tenured faculty; those with the lowest are graduate assistants. Professors working on the West Coast and the East Coast and those working at doctorate-granting institutions also tend to have the highest salaries. Many professors try to increase their earnings by completing research, publishing in their field, or teaching additional courses.

Benefits for full-time faculty typically include health insurance and retirement funds and, in some cases, stipends for travel related to research, housing allowances, and tuition waivers for dependents.

WORK ENVIRONMENT

A college or university is usually a pleasant place in which to work. Campuses bustle with all types of activities and events, stimulating ideas, and a young, energetic population. Much prestige comes with success as a professor and scholar; professors have the respect of students, colleagues, and others in their community.

Depending on the size of the department, college geology professors may have their own office, or they may have to share an office with one or more colleagues. Their department may provide them with a computer, Internet access, and research assistants. College professors are also able to do much of their office work at home. They can arrange their schedule around class hours, academic meetings, and the established office hours when they meet with students. Most college teachers work more than 40 hours each week. Although college professors may teach only two or three classes a semester, they spend many hours preparing for lectures, examining student work, and conducting research.

OUTLOOK

The DOL predicts that employment for college and university professors will grow faster than the average for all careers through 2018. College enrollment is projected to grow due to an increased number of 18- to 24-year-olds, an increased number of adults returning to college, and an increased number of foreign-born students. Retirement of current faculty members will also provide job openings. However, competition for full-time, tenure-track positions at four-year schools will be very strong. More opportunities will be found at community colleges and in high schools.

Geology professors will enjoy steady employment growth through 2018. Opportunities will be best for those who teach environmental geology, engineering geology, and petroleum engineering.

A number of factors threaten to change the way colleges and universities hire faculty. Some university leaders are developing more business-based methods of running their schools, focusing on profits and budgets. This can affect college professors in a number of ways. One of the biggest effects is in the replacement of tenure-track faculty positions with part-time instructors. These part-time instructors include adjunct faculty, visiting professors, and graduate students. Organizations such as the American Association of University Professors and the American Federation of Teachers are working to prevent the loss of these full-time jobs, as well as to help part-time instructors receive better pay and benefits. Other issues involve the development of long-distance education departments in many schools. Though these correspondence courses have become very popular in recent years, many professionals believe that students in long-distance education programs receive only a second-rate education. A related concern is about the proliferation of computers in the classroom. Some courses consist only of instruction by computer software and the Internet. The effects of these alternative methods on the teaching profession will be offset somewhat by the expected increases in college enrollment in coming years.

FOR MORE INFORMATION

To read about the issues affecting college professors, contact the following organizations:

American Association of University Professors
1133 19th Street, NW, Suite 200
Washington, DC 20036-3655
Tel: 202-737-5900
E-mail: aaup@aaup.org
http://www.aaup.org

American Federation of Teachers
555 New Jersey Avenue, NW
Washington, DC 20001-2029
Tel: 202-879-4400
http://www.aft.org

The association represents the interests of women in higher education. Visit its Web site for information on scholarships for college students and AAUW Outlook.

American Association of University Women (AAUW)
1111 16th Street, NW
Washington, DC 20036-4809
Tel: 800-326-2289
E-mail: connect@aauw.org
http://www.aauw.org

For information on careers in geology, contact the following organizations:
American Geological Institute
4220 King Street
Alexandria, VA 22302-1502
Tel: 703-379-2480
http://www.agiweb.org

Geological Society of America
PO Box 9140
Boulder, CO 80301-9140
Tel: 888-443-4472
E-mail: gsaservice@geosociety.org
http://www.geosociety.org

For information on science education, contact the following organizations:
National Association of Geoscience Teachers
c/o Carleton College
B-SERC One North College Street
Northfield, MN 55057-4001
Tel: 507-222-5634
http://www.nagt.org

National Science Teachers Association
1840 Wilson Boulevard
Arlington VA 22201-3092
Tel: 703-243-7100
http://www.nsta.org

INTERVIEW

Dr. Stephen Marshak is a professor of geology and the director of the School of Earth, Society, & Environment at the University of

Illinois in Urbana, Illinois. He discussed his career and the field of geology with the editors of Careers in Focus: Geology.

Q. Can you please tell us about your program and your background?

A. The School of Earth, Society, and Environment (SESE) at the University of Illinois includes three departments (Geology, Geography, and Atmospheric Sciences) each of which hosts its own major, grad program (M.S. and Ph.D.), and research program. SESE also is the anchor for an undergraduate environmental studies major, and for an online environment and sustainability major.

I am a professor in the geology department (my 28th year), and am the director of SESE. I received my A.B. from Cornell, M.S. from Arizona, and Ph.D. from Columbia. My research and teaching specialty area is structural geology, tectonics, and field geology. In addition to courses in these areas, I have also taught introductory geology. My research has involved field studies in North America, South America, Europe, and Antarctica. I have published about 60 research papers, and have advised about 25 graduate students, including several who are now professors elsewhere. As a hobby, I write geology textbooks. So far, I am the author of five, including *Earth: Portrait of a Planet; Essentials of Geology; Earth Structure; Basic Methods of Structural Geology;* and *Laboratory Manual for Introductory Geology.*

Q. What is one thing that young people may not know about a career in geology?

A. There are a great variety of opportunities in the real world, outside of academia and government. Most geologists, in fact, are employed by energy companies, mineral-exploration companies, and geotechnical consulting firms. Starting salaries for some of these geologists can be more than for business majors. Academic geologists work on important problems such as the cause of earthquakes, the processes by which volcanoes erupt, the long-term record of climate change, and the origin of mountains (on Earth and on other planets). Industry geologists are the people who find energy resources and mineral resources, address environmental problems on the landscape and underground, and study the stability and evolution of landscapes.

Q. What do you like most and least about being a geology professor and director of the School of Earth, Society & Environment?

A. Most: Working with students and learning new things. Least: Too little time to get everything done.

Q. What advice would you offer geology majors as they graduate and look for jobs?

A. Though B.S. geologists can have rewarding careers, the M.S. degree is considered to be the professional degree for geologists. Thus, consider graduate school.

Q. What has been one of your most rewarding experiences as an educator, and why?

A. Watching a student's expression when he or she suddenly understands a new concept, and becomes able to read the history of this planet in its rocks and landscapes.

Engineering Geologists

QUICK FACTS

School Subjects
Earth science
Geography
Mathematics

Personal Skills
Mechanical/manipulative
Technical/scientific

Work Environment
Indoors and outdoors
Primarily multiple locations

Minimum Education Level
Bachelor's degree

Salary Range
$43,820 to $82,500 to
$160,910+

Certification or Licensing
Voluntary (certification)
Required by certain states
(licensing)

Outlook
Faster than the average

DOT
024, 055

GOE
02.02.01, 02.07.04

NOC
2113, 2131

O*NET-SOC
17-2051.00, 19-2042.00

OVERVIEW

Geologists study all aspects of the earth, including its origin, history, composition, and structure. *Engineering geologists* are specialized geologists who apply their expertise in geology to identify, prevent, and address geological hazards that arise during the construction of roads, buildings, bridges, dams, and other structures. They are also known as *geological engineers* and *geotechnical engineers*.

HISTORY

During the early years of the United States, geologists and civil engineers in private practice and those working for the U.S. Army Corps of Engineers and other government agencies were often consulted when major construction projects were undertaken to build roads, dams, aqueducts, railroads, tunnels, canals, and buildings. But it was not until the early 1900s that applied geology became recognized as a distinct subfield of geology. According to *The Heritage of Engineering Geology: The First Hundred Years* (Geology Society of America Centennial Special Volume 3, 1991), the Economic Geology Publishing Company was the first professional organization to represent the interests of engineering geologists. It was founded in 1905. Around this time, engineering geology classes began to be offered at U.S. colleges and universities. Two of the first textbooks to reference or focus on engineering geology were *Mineral Deposits* (1913) and *Engineering Geology* (1914).

Geological Hazards

According to the Association of Environmental and Engineering Geologists, engineering geology is the "application of geologic principles to understand, prevent, and mitigate geologic hazards." Following are some of the major geological hazards encountered by engineering geologists:

- Earthquakes
- Erosion
- Expansive and collapsible soils
- Landslides
- Land Subsidence
- Tsunamis
- Volcanoes

Source: Association of Environmental and Engineering Geologists

During the 1930s and 1940s, engineering geology became a respected subfield of geology as a result of strong support from professional geology associations, such as the Geological Society of America, and government agencies, such as the U.S. Army Corps of Engineers, the Bureau of Reclamation, and the Tennessee Valley Authority, as well as state-level agencies. In 1947, the GSA created an Engineering Geology Division for its members. In 1960, the Association of Environmental and Engineering Geologists was founded to represent the professional interests of engineering geologists.

THE JOB

Engineering geologists identify and suggest solutions for geological hazards that may affect the construction of roads, bridges, dams, buildings, and even refuge heaps, among other projects. They combine knowledge of geology with the principles of engineering analysis and design to determine if a particular location is appropriate for the project at hand. They study landforms and identify any potential geological hazards (such as earthquakes and erosion) that might affect construction of a structure and the safety of the people who live in it or use it. If problems are identified, engineering geologists suggest alternatives or changes to the structure's design and construction materials.

When working on a new project, engineering geologists first conduct research as to the site selection. For example, if they are working on a new highway project, engineering geologists consult geological maps, aerial photographs, and other resources to obtain a general idea of the location and its immediate surroundings. They conduct additional research—using industry data, governmental findings, and other sources—to learn as much about the area as possible. Then engineering geologists conduct a field investigation of the site. They may lead and supervise a team of drilling engineers and other workers who collect soil and rock by drilling into the ground or taking samples from the surface. If the proposed site is located near a water source, water samples are collected as well. Once the data is collected, engineering geologists analyze the samples and prepare a report that summarizes the viability of the project from a geological engineering standpoint.

Engineering geologists must also consider naturally occurring phenomena, such as earthquakes, landslides, or flooding, that may affect the project. If a project is located in an area that is flood-prone, for example, the project is not necessarily cancelled, but additional building requirements, different materials, or other precautions are implemented to prevent possible catastrophe.

Once the site is selected and approved, engineering geologists advise architects and construction managers regarding construction materials and methods that are best suited for the location. For example, if a building project is planned for Southern California (which has high earthquake activity), they may suggest that builders use a particular type of coupling beam, such as steel reinforced concrete that would enable the building to better withstand seismic activity.

Engineering geologists also conduct tests on construction materials (such as sand, gravel, bricks, and clay) to determine their strength and durability. They may also be called upon by building managers and planners to help create the project's building budget.

Engineering geologists stay involved throughout the course of a construction project. They may be asked to assume technical control of the site during the duration of the project. At times, they may be asked to provide additional information to clients, government regulatory agencies, or private citizens who will be affected by the project.

Some engineering geologists have managerial duties such as hiring and firing employees, scheduling work shifts, and setting and

An engineering geologist (left) and a surveyor discuss engineering plans to protect a stream. *(Ron Nichols, Natural Resources Conservation Service)*

following budgets. Others teach at colleges and universities and write books and articles about the field.

REQUIREMENTS

High School

The best way to prepare for a career as an engineering geologist is to take a college preparatory curriculum in high school. Science and math classes are the most important to take, especially earth science, chemistry, and physics. Math classes should include algebra, trigonometry, statistics, and calculus, if possible. You should also take courses in computer science, computer-aided design, government, English, and geography.

Postsecondary Training

You will need at least a bachelor's degree in geology or engineering to work as an engineering geologist. Most top positions require a master's degree. Many engineering geologists earn graduate degrees in engineering geology, geophysical technology, geophysical engineering, geology, or engineering. During graduate study, they take classes that focus on hydrology, soil mechanics, geotechnical construction, and rock mechanics, among other topics. The Association of Environmental and Engineering Geologists offers a list of colleges and universities that offer educational programs in geological engineering, geology, hydrogeology, and other geoscience-related programs at its Web site, http://www.aegweb.org.

Engineering geologists also stay current regarding advances in their field by participating in continuing education, conferences, or industry meetings.

Certification or Licensing

The American Institute of Professional Geologists (AIPG) grants the certified professional geologist (CPG) designation to geologists who have earned a bachelor's degree or higher in the geological sciences and have eight years of professional experience (applicants with a master's degree need only seven years of professional experience and those with a Ph.D., five years). Candidates must also undergo peer review by three professional geologists (two of whom must be CPGs) and pay an application fee.

The institute also offers the member designation to geologists who are registered in various states and are not seeking AIPG certification. Applicants must have at least a bachelor's degree in the geological sciences with at least 30 semester hours of geology, be licensed by the state they wish to work in, undergo peer review, and pay an application fee.

More than 30 states require geologists to be registered or licensed. Most of these states require applicants (who have earned a bachelor's degree in the geological sciences) to pass the Fundamentals of Geology exam, a standardized written exam developed by the National Association of State Boards of Geology.

The states of California, Oregon, and Washington require engineering geologists to be licensed. Contact these states' departments of professional regulation for more information on licensing requirements.

Other Requirements

To be a successful engineering geologist, you should have good technical skills, be able to work as a member of a team, enjoy solving problems, and be able to work well under pressure. Strong oral and written communication skills are also important since engineering geologists frequently interact with technicians, civil engineers, architects, scientists, and other engineering geologists. They also spend considerable time writing reports.

EXPLORING

Read books about engineering geology to learn more about the field. Here are two suggestions: *Foundations of Engineering Geology*, 3rd edition, by Tony Waltham (Spon Press, 2009) and *Engineering Geology*, 2nd edition, by F. G. Bell (Butterworth-Heinemann, 2007). Ask your school counselor or science teacher to arrange an information interview with an engineering geologist or a geologist. The Association of Environmental and Engineering Geologists offers a Visiting Professional Program that sends engineering geologists to schools to teach students about the field; contact the association for details. Visit the Web sites of professional geology associations and college geology departments. Join amateur geology groups to gain exposure to the field of geology. Finally, consider participating in a geology field camp during your summer vacation. Field camps, which are typically run by college geology departments, allow you to get out in the field and gain hands-on experience in geology. Visit http://geology.com/field-camp.shtml for a list of field camps.

EMPLOYERS

Engineering geologists are employed by construction companies, civil engineering firms, land-use planners, property owners, and companies that provide geological, architectural, and engineering consulting services. Others work for government agencies at the local, state, or federal level. Some engineering geologists are self-employed. Others work as professors at colleges and universities.

STARTING OUT

Many engineering geologists obtain their first jobs via contacts made through internships or networking events. Others find job leads through industry publications and their college's career services office. Additionally, the Association of Environmental and Engineering Geologists offers job listings at its Web site, http://careers.aegweb.org.

ADVANCEMENT

There are few opportunities for advancement for engineering geologists with only a bachelor's degree. Advanced education and on-the-job experience are required to be eligible for top positions—especially managerial ones. A doctorate is required for most college or university teaching positions and is preferred for much research work.

EARNINGS

The U.S. Department of Labor (DOL) reports that the median annual salary for geoscientists was $82,500 in 2010; the top paid 10 percent earned more than $160,910, while the lowest paid 10 percent earned less than $43,820 a year. In the federal government, the average salary for geologists in managerial, supervisory, and nonsupervisory positions was $95,580 a year. Those employed by architectural and engineering companies earned mean annual salaries of $80,460. Those who worked in the oil and gas extraction industries earned $136,270.

Benefits for full-time workers include vacation and sick time, health, and sometimes dental, insurance, and pension or 401(k) plans. Self-employed engineering geologists must provide their own benefits.

WORK ENVIRONMENT

The job is often stressful since the go-ahead for a construction project often hinges on the careful research and professional expertise of engineering geologists. Engineering geologists must be prepared to defend their findings to construction officials who may not be happy that their project has been delayed or even cancelled as a result of their findings.

Travel is a big part of the job, especially for engineering geologists who are employed by international firms. Engineering geologists must travel to project sites to collect samples of rock, soil, or water, as well as supervise ground investigations. Once the project is approved and underway, the engineering geologist may make periodic visits until completion. They also travel to professional conferences, as well as represent their companies at various industry events.

Since data collection may entail digging, climbing rocks and hills, or wading into streams to gather samples, engineering geologists must be physically fit as well as have good endurance.

OUTLOOK

The employment of geologists is expected to grow faster than the average for all occupations through 2018, according to the DOL. Many geologists are expected to retire in the next decade, which will create many new positions. Opportunities are also expected to be strong for engineering geologists since their work directly contributes to our safety, health, and overall well-being. The DOL reports that "an expected increase in highway building and other infrastructure projects will be a source of jobs for engineering geologists." Engineering geologists with advanced degrees and considerable on-the-job experience will have the best job prospects.

FOR MORE INFORMATION

For more information on accredited surveying and engineering programs, contact

Accreditation Board for Engineering and Technology Inc.
111 Market Place, Suite 1050
Baltimore, MD 21202-7116
Tel: 410-347-7700
E-mail: education@abet.org
http://www.abet.org

For information on careers in geology, contact the following organizations:

American Geological Institute
4220 King Street
Alexandria, VA 22302-1502
Tel: 703-379-2480
http://www.agiweb.org

Geological Society of America
PO Box 9140
Boulder, CO 80301-9140
Tel: 888-443-4472
E-mail: gsaservice@geosociety.org
http://www.geosociety.org

For information on civil engineering, contact

American Society of Civil Engineers
1801 Alexander Bell Drive
Reston, VA 20191-4400
Tel: 800-548-2723
http://www.asce.org

For information on educational programs and careers, contact

Association of Environmental and Engineering Geologists
PO Box 460518
Denver, CO 80246-0518
Tel: 303-757-2926

E-mail: aeg@aegweb.org
http://www.aegweb.org

For information about JETS programs, products, and engineering career brochures (in many disciplines), contact
Junior Engineering Technical Society (JETS)
1420 King Street, Suite 405
Alexandria, VA 22314-2750
Tel: 703-548-5387
E-mail: info@jets.org
http://www.jets.org

For information on career opportunities, contact
U.S. Geological Survey
12201 Sunrise Valley Drive
Reston, VA 20192-0002
Tel: 888-275-8747
http://www.usgs.gov

Geochemists

OVERVIEW

Chemists are scientists who study the composition, changes, reactions, and transformations of matter. *Geochemists* are specialized chemists who study various chemical elements found in the earth's rocks, minerals, soil, and water. Approximately 84,300 chemists are employed in the United States. Only a small number of chemists specialize in geochemistry.

HISTORY

Geochemistry, like geology, is a relatively young discipline. Although the term *geochemistry* was first used by Swiss chemist C. F. Schönbein in 1813 and geologists such as Lardner Vanuxem, Henry D. Rogers, and James Dana made important discoveries regarding the links between chemistry and geology in the first half of the 19th century, it was not until the late 1800s that the subdiscipline of geochemistry evolved as a result of scientific collaboration between physical chemists and geologists.

In 1884, the U.S. Geological Survey established a laboratory to study the chemical makeup of the earth. Another landmark event in the history of geochemistry was the establishment of the Geophysical Laboratory by the Carnegie Institution of Washington in 1905.

Victor Goldschmidt is considered the "father of modern geochemistry." The Swiss mineralogist is best known for his eight-volume *The Geochemical Laws of the Distribution of the Elements*, which laid the foundation for modern geochemistry, and the Goldschmidt Classification of Elements, a geochemical classification of the elements.

Learn More About It

Camenson, Blythe. *Great Jobs for Geology Majors.* 2d ed. New York: McGraw-Hill, 2006.

Chernicoff, Stanley, and Donna Whitney. *Geology.* 4th ed. Upper Saddle River, N.J.: Prentice Hall, 2006.

Ludman, Allan, and Stephen Marshak. *Laboratory Manual for Introductory Geology.* New York: W.W. Norton & Company, 2010.

Lutgens, Frederick K., Edward J. Tarbuck, and Dennis Tasa. *Essentials of Geology.* 10th ed. Upper Saddle River, N.J.: Prentice Hall, 2008.

Marshak, Stephen. *Essentials of Geology.* 3d ed. New York: W. W. Norton & Company, 2009.

McIvor, Don. *Curiosity's Destinations: Tales & Insights from the Life of a Geologist.* Greenwich, Conn.: Grindstone Press, 2005.

Williams, Linda. *Earth Science Demystified.* New York: McGraw-Hill Professional, 2008.

Today, The Geochemical Society represents the professional interests of geochemists.

THE JOB

Geochemists are interested in the chemical puzzles that are found within the earth's rocks, soils, and waters. Not only do they identify the types of minerals and chemical compositions that are present; they also often determine scientific and industrial applications for these resources. Their research is used by oil companies that are drilling for new energy sources; by mining companies that are seeking to reduce the negative impact of their mining activities on the environment; by environmental agencies tasked with disposing of toxic chemicals; and by scientific agencies that seek to understand the structure of geological layers when assessing the severity of earthquakes.

There are several subspecialties within the field of geochemistry. *Isotope geochemists* study the distribution and movement of the earth's elements and their isotopes (different types of atoms from the same chemical element). In this subspecialty, geochemists research changes in, among others, the earth's crust, mantle, and hydrosphere.

Biogeochemists study the effect of chemical biological, physical, and geological processes on the natural world. Some examples of research topics in this field include the eutrophication (overfertilization) of surface waters resulting from pollution; the impact of climate change as a result of chemical and biological changes in the air, water, and soil of the earth; and the feasibility of developing carbon sequestration programs to attempt to reduce global warming.

Organic geochemists study the impact organisms have on the earth. This subspecialty covers a broad area, including sedimentary organic matter and carbon in various forms.

When working on an environmental impact study of abandoned mine wastes, for example, geochemists travel to the location of the mine. During the construction of mines, and all during the mining process, minerals that were once buried in the earth are slowly exposed. Mixing with oxygen in our atmosphere and water from rain and snow, these minerals break down and seep into the water supply—sometimes causing harmful effects to humans and the environment. At the mine site, geochemists collect samples from land piles around the mine to determine if toxic waste has seeped onto the surrounding area. A variety of tests are conducted on these samples. For example, leach studies are conducted to determine the makeup of the rock and if any of their elements have had adverse effects on the water supply. Geochemists use special software programs to create computerized models of hydrocarbon generation and other chemical reactions. Water samples are also tested to measure their acidity levels and heavy metal content. Geochemists are also responsible for mapping specific areas for further geochemical research and analysis.

Geochemists conduct further tests in the laboratory. Geochemists analyze geological samples to gauge their age, chemical composition, radioactivity, and other qualities. Once the tests are conducted and results interpreted, geochemists may need to conduct further field studies.

Geochemists usually work as part of a team of scientists that includes geologists, petroleum engineers, hydrologists, and geophysicists. They may also provide consulting services to government agencies and private corporations.

Many geochemists teach at colleges and universities. Others give presentations at conferences and industry meetings. Some geochemists participate in long-range applied research projects or contribute technical reports and papers to industry journals. All geochemists stay up-to-date on technical developments and research within their industry by attending conferences, reading journals, and joining professional organizations.

REQUIREMENTS

High School

If you are interested in a career in geochemistry, begin preparing in high school by taking advanced-level courses in the physical sciences, mathematics, and English. At least a year each of physics, chemistry (especially analytical chemistry), earth science, and biology is essential, as are the abilities to read graphs and charts, perform difficult mathematical calculations, and write scientific reports. Computer science courses are also important to take, since much of your documentation and other work will involve using computers.

Postsecondary Training

The minimum educational requirement for a career as a geochemist is a bachelor's degree in chemistry, physics, mathematics, oceanography, or geology. The American Chemical Society says that most geochemists have master's degrees in geochemistry, with considerable coursework in analytical, physical, and environmental chemistry. A Ph.D. is recommended for those who are interested in becoming professors and for those seeking employment in consulting firms that specialize in solving geochemical problems. It is not always necessary for employment at government agencies such as the Environmental Protection Agency or the U.S. Geological Survey.

Other Requirements

Geochemists must be detail-oriented, precise workers. They often work with minute quantities, taking minute measurements. They must record all details and reaction changes that may seem insignificant and unimportant to the untrained observer. They must keep careful records of their work and have the patience to repeat experiments over and over again, perhaps varying the conditions in only a small way each time. They should be inquisitive, enjoy solving problems, and have an interest in what makes things work and how things fit together. Geochemists may work alone or in groups. A successful geochemist is not only self-motivated but should be a team player and have good written and oral communication skills.

EXPLORING

The best means of exploring a career in chemistry while still in high school is to pay attention and work hard in chemistry class. This will give you the opportunity to learn the scientific method, perform chemical experiments, and become familiar with chemical terminology. Advanced placement courses will also help. Contact the department of chemistry at a local college or university to discuss the field and arrange tours of their laboratories or classrooms. Due to the extensive training involved, it is very unlikely that a high school student will be able to get a summer job or internship working in a laboratory. However, you may want to contact local manufacturers or research institutions to explore the possibility. Ask your chemistry teacher or a school counselor to arrange an information interview with a chemist or geochemist. Finally, read professional publications about geochemistry such as *Geochemical News* (http://www.geochemsoc.org/publications/geochemicalnews) and *Elements* (http://www.geochemsoc.org/publications/elementsmagazine). Although they are written for geochemists, scanning their pages will give you a general introduction to the field.

EMPLOYERS

Approximately 84,300 chemists are employed in the United States. Only a small percentage specialize in geochemistry. Government agencies—including the U.S. Department of Energy, the Environmental Protection Agency, and the U.S. Geological Service—offer the most positions for geochemists. In the private sector, they work for environmental management and consulting firms, private laboratories, oceanographic institutes, oil companies, mining companies, and colleges and universities.

STARTING OUT

Once you have a degree in chemistry or geochemistry, job opportunities will begin to become available. Summer jobs may become available after your sophomore or junior year of college. You can attend chemical trade fairs and science and engineering fairs to meet and perhaps interview prospective employers. Professors or faculty advisers may know of job openings, and you can begin breaking into the field by using these connections.

The Internet can also be a good source of job leads. Professional organizations often offer job listings at their Web sites. The Geochemical Society, for example, has an online Career Center (http://www.geochemsoc.org/careercenter) that provides job listings.

ADVANCEMENT

In nonacademic careers, advancement usually takes the form of increased job responsibilities accompanied by salary increases. For example, a geochemist may rise from doing basic research in a laboratory to being a group leader, overseeing and directing the work of others. Some geochemists eventually leave the laboratory and set up their own consulting businesses, serving the needs of private companies or government agencies. Others may accept university faculty positions.

Geochemists who work in a university setting follow the advancement procedures for that institution. Typically, a geochemist in academia with a doctoral degree will go from instructor to assistant professor to associate professor and finally to full professor. In order to advance through these ranks, faculty members at most colleges and universities are expected to perform original research and publish their papers in scientific journals of chemistry, geochemistry, and/or other sciences. As the rank of faculty members increases, so do their duties, salaries, responsibilities, and reputations.

EARNINGS

Salary levels for chemists vary based on education, experience, and the area in which they work. According to the U.S. Department of Labor (DOL), median annual earnings for all chemists were $68,320 in 2010. The lowest paid 10 percent earned less than $39,250, and the highest paid 10 percent made more than $116,130 annually. Chemists working for the federal government had mean incomes of $104,210. Those employed in the oil and gas extraction industries earned $105,960.

According to the ACS salary survey of 2009, members with Ph.D.'s earned median annual salaries of $100,000; with master's degrees, $81,000, and with bachelor's degrees, $66,700.

As highly trained, full-time professionals, most geochemists receive health insurance, paid vacations, and sick leave. The specifics of these benefits vary from employer to employer. Geochemists who teach at the college or university level usually work on an academic calendar, which means they get extensive breaks from teaching classes during summer and winter recesses.

WORK ENVIRONMENT

It's hard to pinpoint an average workweek for geochemists. Their schedules and work settings vary by project. Although geochemists spend some time in laboratories, they conduct much of their work outdoors, in all kinds of weather. Some fieldwork may entail traveling to remote and even dangerous locations in order to gather rock, soil, and water samples. Or they may be required to travel to an abandoned mine site. Other projects may require geochemists to wade in shallow streams to collect samples, or travel by boat to conduct experiments on the ocean floor or the shore of a lake. Field-work can be strenuous. Oftentimes, geochemists must climb rocky hills on foot while carrying heavy equipment in their knapsacks. Geochemists wear protective clothing appropriate for the rugged terrain, including sturdy hiking boots and heavy gloves.

Geochemists who are employed by government agencies usually work a traditional 40-hour week. Those employed by private industry often work longer hours, and must be available on weekends to respond to emergencies.

OUTLOOK

The DOL predicts that employment for chemists will grow more slowly than the average for all occupations through 2018. Employment for geochemists will be extremely competitive, but new positions are expected to become available as a result of the strong growth of the oil industry and increased government legislation that seeks to protect the environment. The American Chemical Society reports that geochemists employed in environmental management will have good job prospects. Geochemists with advanced degrees and interdisciplinary experience and education will have the best prospects.

Those wishing to teach full time at the university or college level should find opportunities but also stiff competition. Many of these institutions are choosing to hire people for adjunct faculty positions (part-time positions without benefits) instead of for full-time, tenure-track positions. Nevertheless, a well-trained geochemist should have little trouble finding some type of employment.

FOR MORE INFORMATION

Visit the association's Web site for information on careers and membership for college students, as well as answers to frequently asked questions about the field.
American Association of Petroleum Geologists
PO Box 979
Tulsa, OK 74101-0979
Tel: 800-364-2274
http://www.aapg.org

For information about geochemistry careers and approved education programs, contact

American Chemical Society
1155 16th Street, NW
Washington, DC 20036-4801
Tel: 800-227-5558
http://portal.acs.org

For information about careers in geology, contact the following organizations:

American Geological Institute
4220 King Street
Alexandria, VA 22302-1502
Tel: 703-379-2480
http://www.agiweb.org

Geological Society of America
PO Box 9140
Boulder, CO 80301-9140
Tel: 888-443-4472
E-mail: gsaservice@geosociety.org
http://www.geosociety.org

For information on geochemistry, contact

The Geochemical Society
One Brookings Drive, CB 1169
St. Louis, MO 63130-4899
Tel: 314-935-4131
E-mail: gsoffice@geochemsoc.org
http://www.geochemsoc.org

For information on career opportunities, contact

U.S. Geological Survey
12201 Sunrise Valley Drive
Reston, VA 20192-0002
Tel: 888-275-8747
http://www.usgs.gov

Geographers

OVERVIEW

Geographers study the distribution of physical and cultural phenomena on local, regional, continental, and global scales. There are approximately 1,300 geographers employed in the United States.

HISTORY

The study of geography developed as people tried to understand their world and answer questions about the size, shape, and scope of the earth.

The ancient Greeks made many contributions to early geography. Aristotle denied the widely held belief that the earth was flat and suggested that it had a spherical shape. Later, Eratosthenes calculated the circumference of the earth with remarkable accuracy and developed the concepts of latitude and longitude. Early advances in geography were also made by the Chinese, Egyptians, Arabs, Romans, and others.

Most geographic ideas of the ancient world, including that of the spherical shape of the earth, were lost by Europeans during the Middle Ages. Marco Polo's accounts of his travels in the late 1200s revived interest in geography. Explorations during and after the late 1400s, such as those of Dias, Columbus, da Gama, and Magellan, proved the earth was round and ushered in an age of great discoveries. With it came improved maps and knowledge of the world never before attainable. One of the great mapmakers of the time was Gerhardus Mercator, a 16th-century Flemish geographer.

Richard Hakluyt, an Englishman, and Bernhard Varen, a Dutchman, were notable geographers in the 16th and 17th centuries.

QUICK FACTS

School Subjects
Earth science
Geography

Personal Skills
Helping/teaching
Technical/scientific

Work Environment
Primarily indoors
One location with some travel

Minimum Education Level
Bachelor's degree

Salary Range
$42,450 to $72,800 to $102,440+

Certification or Licensing
Voluntary

Outlook
Much faster than the average

DOT
029

GOE
02.02.01

NOC
4169

O*NET-SOC
19-3092.00

The 18th-century German philosopher Immanuel Kant was one of the first persons to write on the subject matter of geography. Noteworthy geographers of the 19th century included Alexander von Humboldt, Karl Ritter, Friedrich Ratzel, and Albrecht Penck in Germany; Jean Burnhes and Vidal de la Blache in France; Sir Halford Mackinder in Scotland; and William M. Davis in the United States.

Through the years, geography has come to include the study of the earth's surface (that is, the character and structure of an area, including its plant and animal life), as well as the study of economic, political, and cultural life. Thus, the field of geography is concerned with both the physical environment and cultural activities. Some geographers study all these aspects of the earth as they apply to specific regions. More often, however, modern geographers are specialists in one or more subfields of the discipline. These specialists focus on understanding the specific patterns and processes in the physical or human landscape, such as the economic system or the health care delivery system.

THE JOB

Geography can be divided into two broad categories: physical geography and human geography. *Physical geographers* study the processes that create the earth's physical characteristics, such as landforms, soils, vegetation, minerals, water resources, oceans, and weather, and the significance of these processes to humans. *Climatologists* analyze climate patterns and how and why they change. *Geomorphologists*, or *physiographers*, study the origin and development of landforms and interpret their arrangement and distribution over the earth. *Mathematical geographers* study the earth's size, shape, and movements, as well as the effects of the sun, moon, and other heavenly bodies.

Other kinds of physical geographers include *plant geographers, soil geographers*, and *animal geographers*. They study the kinds and distributions of the earth's natural vegetation, soils, and animals. *Cartographers* research data necessary for mapmaking and design and draw the maps. *Computer mappers* are cartographers who use computers and graphics software to draw complex maps.

Human geography is concerned with political organizations, transportation systems, and a wide variety of other cultural activities. *Cultural geographers* study how aspects of geography relate to different cultures. This subspecialty has much in common with archaeology and anthropology.

Regional geographers study all the geographic aspects of a particular area, such as a river basin, an island, a nation, or even an entire continent. They are concerned with the physical, economic, political, and cultural characteristics of the area, and they are often called upon to advise on special problems of the region.

Economic geographers analyze the regional distribution of resources and economic activities, including manufacturing, mining, farming, trade, marketing, and communications.

Medical geographers study how health is affected by our physical setting, including environmental quality. They are interested in the way vegetation, minerals in the water supply, climate, and air pollution affect our health. They may also analyze access to health care by geographic region or setting.

Urban geographers, or *urban and regional planners*, focus on metropolitan problems of a geographic nature. They assist in planning and developing urban and suburban projects, such as residential developments, shopping centers, parking areas, and traffic control systems. They also advise business and industry on plant locations and other geographic issues.

Political geographers study such factors as national boundaries and the relation of natural resources and physical features to local, state, national, and international affairs. They also consult and advise on problems of a geopolitical nature.

Geographic information systems (GIS) is a relatively new, but rapidly growing field. Geographers known as *geographic information system specialists* combine computer graphics, artificial intelligence, and high-speed communications in the mapping, manipulation, storage, and selective retrieval of geographic data. In this way, they are able to display and analyze a wide variety of natural, cultural, and economic information in applications as diverse as worldwide weather forecasting, emergency management, crime prevention, and the monitoring of metropolitan land use. Geographers also use global positioning systems technology, online mapping such as Google Earth, and remote sensing technology to conduct research.

REQUIREMENTS

High School

Plan on continuing your education after high school, so take your school's college prep curriculum. Naturally, you will focus on science classes such as geography and earth science. In addition, you will benefit from taking classes in sociology, computer science, English, history, and mathematics.

Postsecondary Training

A bachelor's degree with a major in geography is the basic educational requirement for most positions as a professional geographer. Advanced degrees are usually required for most college teaching positions and for those opportunities involving a considerable amount of research activity.

Many colleges and universities offer undergraduate programs in geography. A good number of these institutions also have a curriculum leading to a master's degree or doctorate in geography.

Courses taken by geography students include general physical geography; political, economic, human, urban, and regional geography; and specialized courses such as meteorology and cartography. Undergraduate study usually includes formal classroom instruction, as well as some field study.

Certification or Licensing

Geographers who use GIS technology can receive voluntary certification from the GIS Certification Institute. Applicants must meet educational requirements based on a point system, complete coursework and other documented education in GIS and geospatial data technologies, have work experience in a GIS-related position, and participate in conferences or GIS-related events. Applicants who meet the certification requirements may use the certified GIS professional designation. Certification is also offered by the American Society for Photogrammetry and Remote Sensing.

Other Requirements

Prospective geographers need basic skills in statistics and mathematics. They should be able to interpret maps and graphs, express ideas in speech and writing, analyze problems, and make sound judgments.

EXPLORING

There are increasing opportunities to gain experience through college internship programs. A few summer and part-time employment opportunities are available in business or industrial firms. Field experiences, offered as part of the college program, provide the opportunity for potential geographers to test their knowledge and personal qualifications.

You might also want to participate in the National Geography Challenge, which is sponsored by the National Council for Geographic Education. Using a multiple-choice format, you will test your knowledge of geography against students from all over the United States. Ask your geography teacher for more information about the competition.

EMPLOYERS

Approximately 1,300 geographers work in the United States. Many geographers find employment in colleges, universities, and government agencies. Some are employed by business and industrial firms. Most of these positions involve teaching or research responsibilities. A small but growing number of geographers work for map companies, textbook publishers, manufacturers, overseas trading firms, chain stores, market research organizations, real estate developers, environmental consulting firms, travel agencies, banks, and investment firms.

Government agencies that hire geographers include the Central Intelligence Agency, the National Geospatial-Intelligence Agency, the Bureau of Census, and the U.S. Geological Survey. Some geographers work as business consultants, administrators, or planners.

STARTING OUT

Some beginning jobs are available in teaching geography, mostly in secondary schools. However, high school teaching jobs quite often require study in related fields such as social studies, history, or science. Many beginning geographers find positions connected with mapmaking in either government or private industry. Some obtain positions as research or teaching assistants while working toward advanced degrees. Others enter the planning field. Geographers with advanced degrees can qualify for teaching and research positions at the college level. Many consulting jobs also are available.

Each year the federal government offers beginning positions in several geography specialties. Interested students should arrange to take the required civil service examination.

ADVANCEMENT

Advancement is dependent on such factors as amount and type of training, experience, and personal interest and drive. Promotions to jobs requiring more skill and competency are available in all specialty areas. Such jobs are characterized by more administrative, research, or advisory responsibilities in environmental planning.

EARNINGS

Earnings and other benefits depend on the amount of training, the nature of the employment situation, and the personal interests and attributes of the individual employee. According to the U.S. Department of Labor (DOL), median annual earnings for geographers were $72,800 in 2010. Salaries ranged from less than $42,450 annually to more than $102,440.

College and university geography teachers earned salaries that ranged from less than $43,980 to more than $148,970 in 2010, according to the DOL. In addition to salaried income, experienced geographers often earn supplemental incomes through consulting, research, and writing activities. Ph.D.'s in industry frequently earn more than those in academia.

Benefits for full-time workers include vacation and sick time, health, and sometimes dental, insurance, and pension or 401(k) plans. Self-employed geographers must provide their own benefits.

WORK ENVIRONMENT

Geographers usually enjoy pleasant working conditions. They spend much of their time in an office or classroom under the typical working conditions of a business, school, or federal agency.

The average workweek of most geographers is 40 hours, particularly for those employed in government or business positions. In some jobs, however, there can be unusual work situations. Fieldwork often requires the geographer to spend an extended period of time living in remote areas, often under primitive conditions.

OUTLOOK

Geography is a very small profession. With the increased emphasis on planning and research in U.S. business and government, however, the number of geographers is growing. In fact, according to the *Occupational Outlook Handbook*, employment opportunities for geographers are expected to grow much faster than the average for all occupations through 2018. The use of GIS technology in traditional and nontraditional settings, such as emergency services, defense, environmental science, energy exploration, and homeland security, will create many new opportunities for qualified geographers.

Geographers will be needed to analyze or select sites for commercial construction, such as new shopping centers, supermarkets, and industrial parks. There will also be a demand for geographers to work in urban renewal projects, highway programs, real estate development, the telecommunications industry, and environmental planning. Competition for college and university teaching jobs is stiff. Many geographers with graduate degrees seek research and management positions in government and private industry. Others fill nonacademic positions in cartography, health services, climatology, flood management, conservation, and environmental planning.

FOR MORE INFORMATION

For maps, books, journals, and other geography-related materials, contact
American Geographical Society
32 Court Street, Suite 201
Brooklyn, NY 11201-4404
Tel: 718-624-2212
E-mail: AGS@amergeog.org
http://www.amergeog.org

For information on careers in the field, contact
American Society for Photogrammetry and Remote Sensing
5410 Grosvenor Lane, Suite 210
Bethesda, MD 20814-2160
Tel: 301-493-0290
E-mail: asprs@asprs.org
http://www.asprs.org/Geospatial-Job-Opportunities

To order a copy of the publication Careers in Geography, *visit the AAG Web site.*
Association of American Geographers (AAG)
1710 16th Street, NW
Washington, DC 20009-3198
Tel: 202-234-1450
E-mail: gaia@aag.org
http://www.aag.org

Visit the society's Web site to read Cartography and GIS.
Cartography and Geographic Information Society
6 Montgomery Village Avenue, Suite 403
Gaithersburg, MD 20879-3557
Tel: 240-632-9716
http://www.cartogis.org

For more information on certification, contact
GIS Certification Institute
701 Lee Street, Suite 680
Des Plaines, IL 60016-4508
Tel: 847-824-7768
E-mail: info@gisci.org
http://www.gisci.org

For information on geography education, contact
National Council for Geographic Education
1145 17th Street, NW, Room 7620
Washington, DC 20036-4707
Tel: 202-857-7695
http://www.ncge.org

For information on opportunities for women in geography, contact
Society of Women Geographers
415 East Capitol Street, SE
Washington, DC 20003-3810
Tel: 202-546-9228
E-mail: swghq@verizon.net
http://www.iswg.org

For information on career opportunities, contact
U.S. Geological Survey
12201 Sunrise Valley Drive
Reston, VA 20192-0002
Tel: 888-275-8747
http://www.usgs.gov

For information on educational programs in GIS technology,
contact
University Consortium for Geographic Information Science
PO Box 15079
Alexandria, VA 22309-0079
Tel: 703-799-6698
http://ucgis.org

Geographic Information Systems Specialists

OVERVIEW

Geographic information systems specialists create and analyze maps using sophisticated computer systems. GIS specialists in the field of geology help geologists and other geoscientists create maps of geological sites and their components.

HISTORY

Geographic information systems (GIS) have grown up along with the rest of the computer industry in the past 30 to 35 years and have been pushed along particularly in the last 10 years by aggressive GIS software developers, extensive research and development, and widespread application of GIS in many different fields, including civil engineering, public works, surveying, conservation, mining, petroleum, natural gas, water resources, environmental management, and agriculture.

THE JOB

GIS is basically a computer system that can assemble, store, manipulate, and display spatial data. GIS specialists in the field of geology use this computer technology to combine digital map-making techniques with databases.

QUICK FACTS

School Subjects
Computer science
Earth science
Geography

Personal Skills
Communication/ideas
Technical/scientific

Work Environment
Primarily indoors
Primarily one location

Minimum Education Level
Bachelor's degree

Salary Range
$33,260 to $54,510 to $92,730+

Certification or Licensing
Voluntary

Outlook
Faster than the average

DOT
018, 019

GOE
02.08.03

NOC
2255

O*NET-SOC
17-1021.00

GIS technology provides geologists with the ability to electronically map and interpret the features of a geologic site in three dimensions and present this information in a variety of formats on virtual

Types of Rocks

There are three types of rocks: igneous, sedimentary, and metamorphic.

Igneous rocks are created by the cooling and hardening of magma (molten rock that is located deep inside the earth). They are found often on the earth's surface as a result of being expelled from beneath the ground by volcanoes. These types of rocks are called extrusive igneous rocks. Some igneous rocks remain just below the surface (they are called intrusive igneous rocks). Examples of igneous rocks are obsidian and basalt.

Sedimentary rocks are made up of small pieces of rock, sand, shells, and other materials that are pushed together and cemented to one another. Sedimentary rock is often made up soft layers. It is the only type of rock that contain fossils. Examples of sedimentary rocks are amber, sandstone, anthracite, and limestone.

Metamorphic rocks are rocks that change their properties because of alterations in temperature or pressure. They are formed underground. These rocks often have ribbonlike layers and sometimes have crystals. Any rock can change into a metamorphic rock if it is exposed to these conditions. Examples of metamorphic rocks are slate and marble.

globes (also known as *geobrowsers* and digital globes) such as Google Earth, Microsoft Virtual Earth, and NASA World Wind. Interactive geologic maps built within virtual globes allow users to independently view individual map components (units, faults, etc.), data points, and sample locations with associated metadata (orientation measurements, small-scale structures, outcrop photos, etc.), and related components, like cross sections. Information can be inputted from site visits, existing maps, aerial photographs, on-site photographs, satellite images, and global positioning satellite (GPS) data. Exact coordinates are then created on the map; this is called georeferencing.

GIS technology is used in many industries. One popular application for GIS technology is natural resource management. Research scientists use GIS as part of efforts to build understanding about the natural resources. For example, geologists and other research scientists for the U.S. Geological Survey gather and study data relating to coastal erosion and pollution, such as along the mid-Atlantic coast, Gulf Coast, and other areas, in order to help them learn how to stop the erosion. This data includes everything from the movement of sediment during storms to wind, wave, and weather patterns. Systems that allow the scientists to pull all the data together and analyze it in different ways are indispensable in such work.

REQUIREMENTS

High School

To prepare for this career while in high school, take a college preparatory program. You will need a strong background in science (chemistry, physics, biology), mathematics (algebra, geometry, trigonometry, and calculus), social studies, and especially computer science (including programming and applications), so take as many of these classes as your school offers. English courses will help you develop your research and writing skills.

Postsecondary Training

You will need at least a bachelor's degree in geography, GIS, planning, engineering, or computer science to work as a GIS specialist. More than 800 colleges and universities offer courses and programs in geographic information science. Visit the University Consortium for Geographic Information Science's Web site, http://www.ucgis .org/Membership/members.asp, for a list of member schools.

While not required, a minor in geology will provide excellent background experience for aspiring GIS professionals who want to work in the field of geology.

GIS specialists must be proficient with GIS software. One of the most popular software programs for GIS specialists is ArcGIS. Some companies also create proprietary software for their specific needs. In this instance, GIS specialists learn how to use this software after they are hired.

GIS specialists also need skills in report writing, technical support, and teaching/training.

Certification or Licensing

GIS specialists can receive voluntary certification from the GIS Certification Institute. Applicants must have a baccalaureate degree in any field, complete coursework and other documented education in GIS and geospatial data technologies, have work experience in a GIS-related position, and participate in conferences or GIS-related events. Applicants who meet all certification requirements may use the designation certified GIS professional. Certification must be renewed every five years.

Certification is also offered by the American Society for Photogrammetry and Remote Sensing.

Other Requirements

GIS specialists, naturally, must enjoy using computers and keeping up with technology developments that will affect their work, such as new software and new hardware. They should be detail oriented. Frequently, the projects GIS specialists work on are part of a team effort. These specialists, therefore, should be able to work well with others, meet deadlines, and clearly explain their findings. To keep up with their industry and advance in their jobs, GIS specialists must be committed to lifelong learning. GIS specialists who work in the field must be willing to travel to various sites and be away from home for extended periods of time.

EXPLORING

Learn as much as you can about computers—especially computer software. Experiment with Google Earth, Microsoft Virtual Earth, and NASA World Wind. Read books about GIS technology and software. Although many are textbooks that are geared toward professionals, scanning them can provide you with a good overview of the field. You can also read GIS periodicals such as *GEO World* (http://www.geoplace.com) and *Geospatial Solutions* (http://www.gpsworld.com/gis). Finally, if possible, visit a business that provides or uses GIS and ask questions about the technology. You might also ask your science teacher to arrange an information interview with a GIS specialist.

EMPLOYERS

GIS specialists are employed by companies that provide GIS services to companies and organizations that conduct geological surveys. They are also employed directly by museums, colleges and universities, and government agencies (such as the National Park Service, U.S. Geological Survey, U.S. Fish & Wildlife Service, National Geodetic Survey, Environmental Protection Agency, U.S. Forest Service, National Geospatial-Intelligence Agency, Bureau of Indian Affairs, Bureau of Land Management, Army Corps of Engineers, and Bureau of Reclamation).

STARTING OUT

Look in GIS trade magazines for job opportunities or check with the career services office of your community college, college, or university. Search the Internet for sites that specialize exclusively in GIS employment opportunities.

Many geological professional associations and organizations offer job listings at their Web sites. Additionally, employment sites that provide job listings include Earthworks-jobs.com (http://www.earth works-jobs.com) and GeoCommunity (http://careers.geocomm.com).

ADVANCEMENT

Advancement depends on the specific field and employer. Those working for a GIS company might rise from an analyst or software engineering position to manager, or move over to sales and marketing. Where GIS is applied as part of a professional discipline such as engineering, advanced knowledge of GIS may help a job candidate stand out from the crowd and move ahead in his or her field.

EARNINGS

The U.S. Department of Labor (DOL) classifies the career of GIS specialist under the general category of cartographer. In 2010, median annual earnings for cartographers were $54,510. Salaries ranged from less than $33,260 to $92,730 or more. The DOL reports that cartographers employed by local government earned mean annual salaries of $55,520, while those who worked at the federal level earned $82,980.

Full-time GIS specialists usually receive benefits such as vacation days, sick leave, health and life insurance, and a savings and pension program. Self-employed specialists must provide their own benefits.

WORK ENVIRONMENT

GIS specialists typically work in office settings. Geographic information systems usually consist of PC-based workstations with big screens. (Some applications also are available for Macs, but the majority are for PCs.) In an organization where GIS is used extensively, each person might have a GIS workstation at his or her desk. GIS technology is also being used on jobsites in the form of handheld computers combined with mobile GIS devices such as ArcPad or ArcView software operating on a laptop computer or a tablet personal computer.

OUTLOOK

The DOL predicts that employment in the areas of surveying and mapping will grow faster than the average for all occupations through 2018. The outlook for GIS specialists is strong. GIS maps, drawings, animations, and other cartographic images will allow scientists and researchers to view geographic information in new ways. Variations can be tracked over time and possible future changes can be projected and rendered visually. Environmental planning will be a significant area of growth for GIS technology, and federal and local government agencies will continue to be the primary employers of GIS specialists. Private sector opportunities may see some growth in areas such as health care, real estate, retail marketing, tourism, agriculture, energy, and telecommunications.

FOR MORE INFORMATION

For information on careers in geology, contact the following organizations:

American Geological Institute
4220 King Street
Alexandria, VA 22302-1502
Tel: 703-379-2480
http://www.agiweb.org

Geological Society of America
PO Box 9140
Boulder, CO 80301-9140
Tel: 888-443-4472
E-mail: gsaservice@geosociety.org
http://www.geosociety.org

For information on careers, contact

American Society for Photogrammetry and Remote Sensing
5410 Grosvenor Lane, Suite 210
Bethesda, MD 20814-2160
Tel: 301-493-0290
E-mail: asprs@asprs.org
http://www.asprs.org/Geospatial-Job-Opportunities

For more information on careers in GIS and geography, visit the AAG Web site.

Association of American Geographers (AAG)
1710 16th Street, NW
Washington, DC 20009-3198
Tel: 202-234-1450
E-mail: gaia@aag.org
http://www.aag.org

Visit the society's Web site to read Cartography and GIS.
  Cartography and Geographic Information Society
  6 Montgomery Village Avenue, Suite 403
  Gaithersburg, MD 20879-3557
  Tel: 240-632-9716
  http://www.cartogis.org

For information on employment as a GIS professional in a variety of industries, contact
  Environmental Systems Research Institute
  380 New York Street
  Redlands, CA 92373-8100
  Tel: 800-447-9778
  http://www.esri.com
  http://www.esri.com/industries/map-chart-dataproduction/
    cartography/index.html

For more information on certification, contact
  GIS Certification Institute
  701 Lee Street, Suite 680
  Des Plaines, IL 60016-4508
  Tel: 847-824-7768
  E-mail: info@gisci.org
  http://www.gisci.org

For information on educational program in GIS, contact
  University Consortium for Geographic Information Science
  PO Box 15079
  Alexandria, VA 22309-0079
  Tel: 703-799-6698
  http://ucgis.org

This science agency of the U.S. Department of the Interior has information on geospatial data, publications, education, and more on its Web site.
  U.S. Geological Survey
  12201 Sunrise Valley Drive
  Reston, VA 20192-0002
  Tel: 888-275-8747
  http://www.usgs.gov

The Environmental Systems Research Institute has created the site GIS.com, which provides information on topics such as what GIS is, GIS training, and GIS specialties.
  GIS.com
  http://www.gis.com

Geological Oceanographers

OVERVIEW

Oceanographers study the oceans of the world. *Geological oceanographers* are specialized oceanographers who study the topographic features, geological processes, and physical composition of the ocean bottom. Their work greatly contributes to our knowledge and understanding of earth's geological history, as well as potential changes in the future, through observations, surveys, and experiments. Geological oceanographers are also known as *marine geologists*.

HISTORY

People have always been curious about the geological makeup of the oceans of the world, but serious scientific investigation did not occur until the 20th century because of the lack of technology that would allow scientists to conduct comprehensive research.

The origins of geological oceanography as we know it today can be traced to Project Mohole, an undersea drilling project that recovered the first sample of oceanic crust in 1961. In 1968, the U.S. National Science Foundation organized the Deep Sea Drilling Project (DSDP). The project collected core samples and rocks from the oceans of the world and helped scientists answer a wealth of questions about the geological composition of the ocean floor. Major discoveries included obtaining proof of seafloor renewal at rift zones and continental drift. In 1975, the DSDP was reconstituted as the International Program of Ocean

Drilling (IPOD). Participating countries included the United States, France, the United Kingdom, Japan, the Soviet Union, and the Federal Republic of Germany. In 1985, the Ocean Drilling Program replaced IPOD. Major discoveries, according to the National Science Foundation, included "evidence of fluids circulating through the ridge flanks of the ocean floor, the formation of volcanoes and volcanic plateaus at rates unknown today, natural methane frozen deep within oceanic crust, and persistently rhythmic climate history." In 2003, the United States and Japan launched the Integrated Ocean Drilling Program (IODP). The IODP continues to study the ocean floor, and more discoveries can be expected in the future.

Drilling is not the only research method used by modern geological oceanographers. They also use satellites, sonar, remote-operated vehicles, and a variety of other technologies to explore, study, and map the ocean floor.

THE JOB

Geological oceanographers study the contour and materials of the seafloor (rocks, fossils, etc.) in order to draw conclusions about ocean circulation, climate, seafloor spreading, plate tectonics, and the ocean's geological features. They study physical features such as underwater mountains, rises and ridges, trenches, valleys, abyssal hills, and the ocean crust. They take sediment samples from the ocean floor to learn about the history of oceanic circulation and climates. Geological oceanographers study the physical and chemical properties of sediment samples, as well as their age, distribution, and origin—to learn more about historical and ongoing geological processes. They attempt to understand the origin of volcanoes and earthquakes and the gradual movement of the earth's surface. They also study erosional processes and the formation of hydrothermal vents.

Geological oceanography is considered to be one of the most diverse earth sciences fields, with many subspecialties. Some specializations include seismology, ocean drilling, ocean mining and oil and gas exploration, coastal geology, paleontology, geochronology, and petrology.

Seismologists use sound waves to study the earth's interior structure. They specialize in the study of earthquakes. With the aid of the seismogram and other instruments that record the location of earthquakes and the vibrations they cause, seismologists examine active fault lines and areas where earthquakes have occurred.

Geological oceanographers who specialize in ocean drilling collect soil and rock samples from beneath the ocean floor. One major international drilling project is the Integrated Ocean Drilling Program. According to Sea Grant, marine scientists participating in the program have made many major discoveries. They include "a new understanding of the causes and history of the ice ages, the evolution of the continental margins, earth's tectonic processes, marine sedimentation, and the origin and evolution of the oceanic crust."

Those who specialize in ocean mining and oil and gas exploration search the ocean for potential sources of oil, gas, and minerals (such as manganese nodules that contain manganese, nickel, cobalt, copper; sand and gravel; phosphate; and other minerals).

Coastal geologists study the topographic features, geological processes, and physical composition of coastal regions. They also study effects of human development and nature on these regions. (See the article Geologists for more information.)

Paleontologists specialize in the study of the earth's rock formations, including remains of plant and animal life, in order to understand the earth's evolution and estimate its age. (See the article Paleontologists for more information.)

Geochronologists are geoscientists who use radioactive dating and other techniques to estimate the age of rock and other samples from an exploration site.

Petrologists study the origin and composition of igneous, metamorphic, and sedimentary rocks. (See the article Petrologists for more information.)

Geological oceanographers may spend some of their time on the water each year gathering data and making observations. They do additional oceanographic work on land. Experiments using mathematical modeling software or geological samples may be conducted in a seaside laboratory. They use geographic information systems (GIS) software to create 3-D computer maps of the seafloor. Geological oceanographers also collect data using satellites, seismic techniques, sonar, dredging processes, and, as mentioned earlier, deep-sea drilling projects.

Geological oceanographers usually work as part of a highly skilled, interdisciplinary team, often teaming with biological, chemical, and physical oceanographers and geologists, geophysicists, and other scientists and technicians on projects.

Some geological oceanographers teach at high schools and colleges and universities. Others write textbooks and articles about geological oceanography.

REQUIREMENTS

High School

To prepare for a career as a geological oceanographer, take a college preparatory curriculum that includes math classes, such as algebra, trigonometry, calculus, and statistics, and science courses, including chemistry, biology, and geology. Speech and English will help you hone your communication skills. Computer classes will come in handy since oceanographers use a variety of computer software and hardware to do their work. Taking a foreign language will be useful—especially if you plan to work abroad.

Postsecondary Training

Once in college, prospective geological oceanographers should continue to take science courses, including geology, biology, chemistry, and physics. While some universities do offer undergraduate oceanography programs, students who plan to go on to graduate school should not necessarily major in marine science or oceanography. In fact, most geological oceanographers concentrate on a related area of science, such as geology, chemistry, physics, or biology, before studying geological oceanography in graduate school. A well-rounded background in science is essential to a career as a geological oceanographer.

Students who plan to pursue an advanced degree in oceanography should look for institutions that offer significant hands-on research experience. More than 100 institutions offer programs in marine studies, and more than 35 universities offer graduate programs in oceanography.

Typical classes in a geological oceanography program include Introduction to Geological Oceanography, Marine Geological Processes, Marine Sedimentary Processes, Introduction to Sedimentary Geology, Marine Seismology, Geophysical Continuum Mechanics, and Physics of the Oceanic Lithosphere.

Many oceanography students participate in internships or work as teaching assistants while in college to gain hands on experience in the field. The American Society of Limnology and Oceanography offers a list of internships at its Web site, http://www.aslo.org.

Certification or Licensing

Oceanographers may scuba dive when conducting research. Organizations such as PADI provide basic certification (see For More Information for contact details).

Other Requirements

To succeed as a geological oceanographer, you must be intelligent, willing to work hard and at irregular hours, highly organized, and able to work closely with other people. Oceanographers must have superior computer and math skills. Cooperation is particularly important in this field, since oceanographers must work closely together on research projects. Because oceanographers must publish the results of their research, excellent writing skills are also essential. The most important characteristic for an oceanographer, however, may be intellectual curiosity. Oceanographers must yearn to solve nature's mysteries.

EXPLORING

Read books and visit Web sites about oceanography. One book suggestion: *Oceanography: An Invitation to Marine Science*, 7th edition, by Tom S. Garrison. Your school or community librarian can suggest many other resources. You can also visit Sea Grant's Marine Careers Web site (http://www.marinecareers.net) for information on careers, internships, volunteerships, and other activities, such as sea camps. Visit the Web sites of college oceanography departments, which offer information about the field, lists of typical classes, and details on internships. You may even be able to contact a professor or department head to ask a few questions about the career. Other ways to learn more about the field include asking your science teacher to arrange an information interview with a geological oceanographer and visiting an oceanography research center, such as Woods Hole Oceanographic Institution, or a local aquarium or even a zoo to learn about ocean environments.

EMPLOYERS

Approximately 23 percent of those working in oceanography and marine-related fields work for federal or state governments. Federal employers of geological oceanographers include the National Science Foundation, Departments of Commerce (National Oceanic and Atmospheric Administration), Defense, Energy, and Interior (National Park Service, Minerals Management Service); National Aeronautics and Space Administration; Environmental Protection Agency; Biological Resources Discipline of the U.S. Geological Survey, Naval Oceanographic Office, Naval Research Laboratory, and Office of Naval Research. State governments often employ oceanographers in environmental agencies or state-funded research projects.

Forty percent of oceanographers are employed by colleges or universities, where they teach, conduct research, write, and consult. The remaining oceanographers work for private industries such as oil and gas extraction companies and nonprofit organizations, including environmental societies.

STARTING OUT

Good sources of job leads for recent oceanography graduates include professors, contacts made during internships, and college career services offices. Additionally, the Marine Technology Society, American Society of Limnology and Oceanography, The Oceanography Society, and the Geological Society of America offer job listings at their Web sites.

ADVANCEMENT

Geological oceanographers advance by receiving higher salaries and by assuming administrative responsibilities. They also find work at larger organizations that are engaged in more prestigious research. The normal pattern of advancement for college professors is from instructor to assistant professor, to associate professor, to full professor.

EARNINGS

According to the U.S. Department of Labor (DOL), in 2010, salaries for geoscientists (an occupational group that includes geologists, geophysicists, and oceanographers) ranged from less than $43,820 to more than $160,910, with a median of $82,500. The average salary for oceanographers working for the federal government was $95,580 in March 2010.

Benefits for geological oceanographers depend on the employer; however, they usually include such items as health insurance, retirement or 401(k) plans, and paid vacation days. Oceanographers receive additional earnings from lecturing, consulting, and publishing their findings.

WORK ENVIRONMENT

Geological oceanographers work indoors in offices, laboratories, and classrooms and in outdoor settings such as the deck of a research vessel, a rocky beach, or in a submersible on the ocean floor. Those who conduct field research must be away from their families for long periods and live in close quarters with other marine scientists and support staff. Weather conditions vary greatly. On one expedition, a geological oceanographer may work in or near the icy water of the Arctic, and on another in the hot sun and balmy waters of tropical regions. Geological oceanographers who work as college professors spend only 12 to 16 a week in the actual classroom, but they spend many hours preparing lectures and lesson plans, grading papers and exams, and preparing grade reports. During holiday and summer breaks, they have the opportunity to travel and conduct research.

OUTLOOK

Employment for all geoscientists (including oceanographers) will grow faster than the average for all occupations through 2018, according to the DOL. There is much yet to learn about the geological makeup of the ocean floor, which should translate into continued demand for geological oceanographers. Despite this prediction, competition for top positions will be strong. Those with a Ph.D., who speak a foreign language, and a willingness to work abroad will have the best employment prospects.

As the nations of the world continue to search for new energy reserves and raw materials, opportunities for geological oceanographers who are employed by ocean mining and oil and gas exploration companies will be especially strong. Demand and supply, however, are difficult to predict and can change according to the world market situation; for example, the state of the offshore oil market can affect employment demand.

FOR MORE INFORMATION

For education and career information, contact the following organizations:

Acoustical Society of America
Two Huntington Quadrangle, Suite 1NO1
Melville, NY 11747-4502
Tel: 516-576-2360
E-mail: asa@aip.org
http://acousticalsociety.org

American Geophysical Union
2000 Florida Avenue, NW
Washington, DC 20009-1277

Tel: 800-966-2481
http://www.agu.org

For information on careers in geology and chapters for college students, contact
American Association of Petroleum Geologists
PO Box 979
Tulsa, OK 74101-0979
Tel: 800-364-2274
http://www.aapg.org

For information on geoscience careers, contact
American Geological Institute
4220 King Street
Alexandria, VA 22302-1502
Tel: 703-379-2480
http://www.agiweb.org

For information on careers, contact
American Institute of Professional Geologists
12000 Washington Street, Suite 285
Thornton, CO 80241-3134
Tel: 303-412-6205
E-mail: aipg@aipg.org
http://www.aipg.org

Visit the society's Web site for information on careers and education.
American Society of Limnology and Oceanography
5400 Bosque Boulevard, Suite 680
Waco, TX 76710-4446
Tel: 800-929-2756
E-mail: business@aslo.org
http://www.aslo.org

For career information and profiles of women in geophysics, visit the association's Web site.
Association for Women Geoscientists
12000 Washington Street, Suite 285
Thornton, CO 80241-3134
Tel: 303-412-6219
E-mail: office@awg.org
http://www.awg.org

For information on chapters for college students, contact
Association of Environmental and Engineering Geologists
PO Box 460518
Denver, CO 80246-0518
Tel: 303-757-2926
E-mail: aeg@aegweb.org
http://www.aegweb.org

For career information and job listings, contact
Geological Society of America
PO Box 9140
Boulder, CO 80301-9140
Tel: 888-443-4472
E-mail: gsaservice@geosociety.org
http://www.geosociety.org

For an overview of remote sensing, contact
Geoscience and Remote Sensing Society
Institute of Electrical and Electronics Engineers
445 Hoes Lane
Piscataway, NJ 08854-4141
E-mail: info@ieee-grss.org
http://www.grss-ieee.org

To purchase the booklet Education and Training Programs in Oceanography and Related Fields, *contact*
Marine Technology Society
5565 Sterrett Place, Suite 108
Columbia, MD 21044-2606
Tel: 410-884-5330
https://www.mtsociety.org

For information on oceanography, contact
National Oceanic and Atmospheric Administration
c/o U.S. Department of Commerce
1401 Constitution Avenue, NW, Room 5128
Washington, DC 20230-0001
http://www.noaa.gov

Contact the society for ocean news and information on membership.
The Oceanography Society
PO Box 1931
Rockville, MD 20849-1931

Tel: 301-251-7708
E-mail: info@tos.org
http://www.tos.org

For information on diving instruction and certification, contact
PADI
30151 Tomas Street
Rancho Santa Margarita, CA 92688-2125
Tel: 800-729-7234
http://www.padi.com

For career information and job listings, contact
Seismological Society of America
201 Plaza Professional Building
El Cerrito, CA 94530-4003
Tel: 510-525-5474
E-mail: info@seismosoc.org
http://www.seismosoc.org

For information on careers in geophysics and student chapters at colleges and universities, contact
Society of Exploration Geophysicists
PO Box 702740
Tulsa, OK 74170-2740
Tel: 918-497-5500
http://www.seg.org

To learn more about coastal and marine geology, visit
U.S. Geological Survey: Coastal and Marine Geology Program
http://marine.usgs.gov

For links to career information and sea programs, visit the follow-ing Web sites:
Careers in Oceanography, Marine Science, and Marine Biology
http://ocean.peterbrueggeman.com/career.html

Sea Grant Marine Careers
http://www.marinecareers.net

WomenOceanographers.org
http://www.womenoceanographers.org

Geological Technicians

OVERVIEW

Geological technicians assist geologists in their studies of the earth's physical makeup and history. This includes the exploration of a wide variety of phenomena, such as mountain uplifting, rock formations, mineral deposition, earthquakes, and volcanic eruptions. Modern geology is particularly concerned with the exploration for mineral and petroleum deposits in the earth and with minimizing the effects of human-made structures on the environment.

Petroleum technicians are specialized geological technicians who measure and record the conditions of oil and gas wells. They use instruments lowered into the wells, and evaluate mud from the wells. They examine data to determine petroleum and mineral content.

There are approximately 15,200 geological and petroleum technicians employed in the United States.

HISTORY

Because of our reliance on petroleum and natural gas to help us meet so many of our basic energy needs, many geologists have focused in recent years on the exploration for new deposits of these fossil fuels. Natural gas provides fuel for ovens and for furnaces to heat homes. Petroleum is refined into gasoline for cars, grease to keep machinery parts operating smoothly, and plastic, tar, and kerosene, among other products.

Small companies and large multinational corporations send teams of geologists and drill operators to scour farms, deserts, and the ocean floor for new deposits of oil. One of the most important members on these teams is the geological technician.

THE JOB

Geological technicians most often work under the supervision of a geologist or other geoscientist as part of a research team. Some areas of specialization include *environmental geology*, the study of how pollution, waste, and hazardous materials affect the earth; *geophysics*, the study of the earth's interior and magnetic, electric, and gravitational fields; *hydrology*, the investigation of the movement and quality of surface water; *petroleum geology*, the exploration and production of crude oil and natural gas; and *seismology*, the study of earthquakes and the forces that cause them.

The most common employment for geological technicians is with *petroleum geologists*. These scientists determine where deposits of oil and natural gas may be buried beneath the earth's surface. Using data gathered from workers in the field, geological technicians draft maps displaying where drilling operations are taking place

A geological technician in Antarctica uses a grinding machine to prepare samples for study. He is part of a team that is studying Antarctica's role in global environmental change over the past 65 million years. *(Elaine Hood, NSF/Lightroom/Topfoto/The Image Works)*

and create reports that geologists will use to determine where an oil deposit might be located.

Geological technicians draft maps that pinpoint the exact location where a drilling crew has dug a well. In addition to indicating whether or not oil was found, the map will also specify the depth of the well. If oil is located, the information on the map will enable geologists to determine the probable size of the oil deposit.

Technicians also analyze various types of raw data when creating reports. Crews often, for example, detonate carefully planned explosions that send shock waves deep into the earth. These waves are recorded by microphones. Geologists study the patterns of the waves to determine the composition of rock beneath the surface. Geological technicians take these patterns and remove any background noise, such as sound waves from an airplane passing overhead, and then write a report that summarizes what the sound patterns indicate.

Some geological technicians work in the field of environmental engineering. Assisting geologists, they study how structures, such as roads, landfills, and commercial, residential, and industrial developments, affect the environment. The information they gather is incorporated into environmental impact statements, which are used by developers, government officials, and private land owners to minimize damage to the environment.

REQUIREMENTS

High School
You will need a high school diploma if you are considering a career as a geological technician and hope to advance into supervisory positions. Though some people acquire their skills on the job, it is helpful to begin your preparation in high school.

Courses in geology, geography, and mathematics, including algebra, trigonometry, and statistics, are all recommended. Drafting courses can teach important mapmaking skills, and courses in computer-aided design are useful since many companies now design maps using computer software. Additionally, courses in English and speech will help you develop the communication skills necessary for writing reports and serving as a liaison between geologists and field crews.

Postsecondary Training
Though not required, some postsecondary education may be helpful in finding a job, particularly in the increasingly competitive oil and gas industry. A bachelor of science degree, with an emphasis in geology, advanced mathematics, and drafting, is recommended. Some

companies will not hire technicians without a degree. Some two-year colleges offer an associate's degree in geology or geologic technology.

Other Requirements

In addition to academic preparation, successful technicians are detail oriented and have excellent time management and organizational skills. Drilling for oil, for example, can be a costly and time-consuming venture. Competence in interpreting data is crucial because oil companies and other employers rely heavily on the accuracy of information reported by their geological technicians.

EXPLORING

School counselors and librarians are a good source of information about careers. A science teacher may also be helpful in providing specific information about a career as a geological aide. Large oil and gas companies, such as BP, Chevron, Texaco, and Shell Oil Company, may be able to provide information about careers in the geological sciences, and some of these companies occasionally offer educational programs for high school students and opportunities for summer employment.

In addition to studying geology in school and contacting employers to learn about the profession, you should consider joining a geology-related club or organization, for example, concerned with rock collecting. Local amateur geological groups also offer opportunities to gain exposure to the geological sciences.

EMPLOYERS

Approximately 15,200 geological and petroleum technicians work in the United States. Technicians are employed by major oil and gas companies. Environmental consulting and environmental engineering firms may also be a source of employment in the private sector. With these firms, geological technicians assist in creating environmental impact studies.

The federal government hires geologists and may employ geological technicians in the Department of the Interior (specifically in the U.S. Geological Survey and the Bureau of Reclamation) and in the Departments of Defense, Agriculture, and Commerce.

State agencies, nonprofit research organizations, and state-funded museums are also possible sources of employment for geological technicians.

STARTING OUT

After completing high school or college, the prospective geological technician can look for work in various areas, including private industry and government. The exploration departments of oil and gas companies are the first places to look for a position as a geological technician. Most are multinational corporations and are likely to have many geological technicians on staff in the United States, as well as in overseas departments.

Internships and volunteerships should be considered. Large corporations and professional associations are resources for internship information. Volunteer opportunities are also available.

ADVANCEMENT

Advancement for geological technicians depends on the size of the organization they work for and their educational background. At smaller companies and consulting firms, the range of tasks may be quite varied. Geological technicians may perform some tasks that geologists normally do, as well as some clerical duties. At larger companies, the opposite may be true. A geological technician might specialize in well spotting, for example, or supervise a staff of several geological technicians.

Supervisory positions are often available to technicians with several years of on-the-job experience. Typically, these technicians will train new staff in proper procedures and methods, as well as check their work for accuracy before sending it to the geologist.

With additional education and either a master's degree or doctorate, geological technicians can go on to work as geologists, soil scientists, or paleontologists, for example.

EARNINGS

Geological and petroleum technicians earned salaries that ranged from less than $29,950 to more than $99,860 in 2010, according to the U.S. Department of Labor (DOL). The average salary for these technicians was $54,020. Those who worked in the oil and gas extraction industries earned $65,290.

Depending on their employers, most geological technicians enjoy a full complement of benefits, including vacation and sick time as well as holidays and medical and dental insurance. Self-employed workers must provide their own benefits.

WORK ENVIRONMENT

Geological technicians frequently work out in the field where drilling or testing is occurring. In these situations, aides may spend considerable time outdoors in primitive or rugged conditions. Sometimes this involves camping for several days in a remote location.

Geological technicians who are employed in a laboratory or office generally work regular 40-hour weeks in pleasant conditions. The work each day is fairly routine. It may involve gathering data from the previous day's tests, examining preliminary reports from drilling crews, drafting maps, and writing reports for the geologist.

Geological technicians provide important support to geologists and other geoscientists. They are responsible for the accurate organization and presentation of important data. In a petroleum company, for example, geological technicians are a crucial link in the search to locate hidden pockets of fossil fuel. They shoulder a lot of responsibility for the successful outcome of exploratory drilling operations. While this may at times be stressful, it is also rewarding because geological technicians are able to see tangible results from their work.

OUTLOOK

The DOL predicts that there will be little or no employment change for geological technicians. The outlook for geological technicians is closely linked to the price of oil and natural gas. When prices for these energy resources are high, companies hire more technicians. When they are low, oil and natural gas companies reduce exploration and hire fewer workers.

Geological technicians who are fluent in a foreign language and who are willing to work abroad should enjoy the best opportunities. In addition, job opportunities in environmental consulting will continue to be good as long as environmental regulations remain intact.

Though geological technicians tend to have training that is best suited to their own field, they might find employment with companies that value their mapmaking and computer-aided drafting abilities. Public utility companies, architectural firms, developers, and some private consulting firms might have a need for these skills.

FOR MORE INFORMATION

For information on careers in geology, contact the following organizations:

American Geological Institute
4220 King Street
Alexandria, VA 22302-1502
Tel: 703-379-2480
http://www.agiweb.org

Geological Society of America
PO Box 9140
Boulder, CO 80301-9140
Tel: 888-443-4472
E-mail: gsaservice@geosociety.org
http://www.geosociety.org

For information on the geophysical sciences, contact
American Geophysical Union
2000 Florida Avenue, NW
Washington, DC 20009-1277
Tel: 800-966-2481
http://www.agu.org

For career information and profiles of women in geophysics, visit the AWG Web site.
Association for Women Geoscientists (AWG)
12000 North Washington Street, Suite 285
Thornton, CO 80241-3134
Tel: 303-412-6219
E-mail: office@awg.org
http://www.awg.org

For career and educational information about the geosciences, visit
U.S. Geological Survey
http://education.usgs.gov

Geologists

OVERVIEW

Geologists study all aspects of the earth, including its origin, history, composition, and structure. Along more practical lines, geologists may, through the use of theoretical knowledge and research data, locate groundwater, oil, minerals, and other natural resources. They play an increasingly important role in studying, preserving, and cleaning up the environment. They advise construction companies and government agencies on the suitability of locations being considered for buildings, highways, and other structures. They also prepare geological reports, maps, and diagrams. There are approximately 33,600 geoscientists (which includes geologists, geophysicists, and oceanographers) employed in the United States.

HISTORY

Geology is a young science, first developed by early mining engineers. In the late 18th century, scientists such as A. G. Werner and James Hutton, a retired British physician, created a sensation with their differing theories on the origins of rocks. Through the study of fossils and the development of geological maps, others continued to examine the history of the earth in the 19th century.

From these beginnings, geology has made rapid advances, both in scope and knowledge. With the development of more intricate technology, geologists are able to study areas of the earth they were previously unable to reach. Seismographs, for example, measure energy waves resulting from the earth's movement in order to determine the location and intensity

A geologist chips at ore deep inside a mine. His work will provide guidance to miners as they blast into the ore reserve. *(James Woodcock, AP Photo/Billings Gazette)*

of earthquakes. Seismic prospecting involves bouncing sound waves off buried rock layers.

THE JOB

The geologist's work includes locating and obtaining physical data and material. This may necessitate the drilling of deep holes to obtain samples, the collection and examination of the materials found on or under the earth's surface, or the use of instruments to measure the earth's gravity and magnetic field. Some geologists may spend three to six months of each year conducting fieldwork. In laboratory work, geologists carry out studies based on field research. Sometimes working under controlled temperatures or pressures, geologists analyze the chemical and physical properties of geological specimens, such as rock, fossil remains, and soil. Once the data is analyzed and the studies are completed, geologists and geological technicians write reports based on their research.

A wide variety of laboratory instruments are used, including X-ray diffractometers, which determine the crystal structure of minerals, and petrographic microscopes for the study of rock and sediment samples.

Profile: Louis Agassiz (1807–73)

Louis Agassiz was a Swiss paleontologist, glaciologist, and geologist. He is known as one of the "founding fathers of the modern American scientific tradition," according to the University of California Museum of Paleontology. Agassiz was one of the first scientists to study the earth's natural history. He taught natural history at many elite schools in Europe and the United States, including the University of Neuchâtel and Harvard University. Agassiz was instrumental in the founding of the John Anderson School in Massachusetts, a school that specialized in marine zoology.

Agassiz is best known as one of the originators of the glacial theory, which postulated that ice covered large areas of the earth's surface in the past. Scientists have proven that this is true, with the earth going through various ice ages during its history. Agassiz is also known for being a lifelong opponent of Charles Darwin's theory of evolution.

Agassiz died in 1873, and is buried at Mount Auburn Cemetery, Cambridge, Massachusetts.

Sources: *The Encyclopedia of Earth*, University of California Museum of Paleontology

Geologists working to protect the environment may design and monitor waste disposal sites, preserve water supplies, and reclaim contaminated land and water to comply with federal environmental regulations.

Geologists often specialize in one of the following disciplines in the two main branches of the field: physical geology and historical geology.

Physical Geology

Economic geologists search for new resources of minerals and fuels. *Petroleum geologists* are economic geologists who attempt to locate natural gas and oil deposits through exploratory testing and study of the data obtained. They recommend the acquisition of new properties and the retention or release of properties already owned by their companies. They also estimate oil reserves and assist petroleum engineers in determining exact production procedures.

Engineering geologists are responsible for the application of geological knowledge to problems arising in the construction of roads, buildings, bridges, dams, and other structures. (See the article Engineering Geologists for more information.)

Environmental geologists study how pollution, waste, hazardous materials, and flooding and erosion affect the earth.

Geohydrologists, also known as *hydrogeologists*, study the nature and distribution of water within the earth and are often involved in environmental impact studies.

Geomorphologists study the form of the earth's surface and the processes, such as erosion and glaciation, that bring about changes.

Geophysicists are concerned with matter and energy and how they interact. They study the physical properties and structure of the earth, from its interior to its upper atmosphere, including land surfaces, subsurfaces, and bodies of water.

Glacial geologists study the physical properties and movement of ice sheets and glaciers.

Marine geologists study the oceans, including the seabed and subsurface features. They are also known as *geological oceanographers*. (See the article Geological Oceanographers for more information.)

Mineralogists are interested in the classification of minerals composing rocks and mineral deposits. To this end, they examine and analyze the physical and chemical properties of minerals and precious stones to develop data and theories on their origin, occurrence, and possible uses in industry and commerce.

Petrologists study the origin and composition of igneous, metamorphic, and sedimentary rocks. (See the article Petrologists for more information.)

Seismologists study earthquake shocks and their effects.

Structural geologists investigate the stresses and strains in the earth's crust and the deformations they produce.

The geologist is far from limited in a choice of work, but a basic knowledge of all sciences is essential in each of these specializations. An increasing number of scientists combine geology with detailed knowledge in another field. Geochemists, for example, are concerned with the chemical composition of, and the changes in, minerals and rocks, while planetary geologists apply their knowledge of geology to interpret surface conditions on other planets and the moon. (See the article Geochemists for more information.)

Historical Geology

Geochronologists are geoscientists who use radioactive dating and other techniques to estimate the age of rock and other samples from an exploration site.

Paleontologists specialize in the study of the earth's rock formations, including remains of plant and animal life, in order to understand the earth's evolution and estimate its age. (See the article Paleontologists for more information.)

Sedimentologists, also known as sedimentary geologists, study sediments such silt, sand, and mud. These sediments often contain coal, gas, oil, and mineral deposits. Closely related to sedimentologists are *stratigraphers.* Stratigraphers study the distribution and relative arrangement of sedimentary rock layers. This enables them to understand evolutionary changes in fossils and plants, which leads to an understanding of successive changes in the distribution of land and sea.

REQUIREMENTS

High School

Because you will need a college degree in order to find work in this profession, you should take a college preparatory curriculum while in high school. Such a curriculum will include computer science, history, English, and geography classes. Science and math classes are also important to take, particularly earth science, chemistry, and physics. Math classes should include algebra, trigonometry, and statistics.

Postsecondary Training

A bachelor's degree is the minimum requirement for entry into lower-level geology jobs, but a master's degree is usually necessary for beginning positions in research, teaching, and exploration. A person with a strong background in physics, chemistry, mathematics, or computer science may also qualify for some geology jobs. For those wishing to make significant advancements in research and in teaching at the college level, a doctoral degree is required. Those interested in the geological profession should have an aptitude not only for geology but also for physics, chemistry, and mathematics.

A number of colleges, universities, and institutions of technology offer degrees in geology. Programs in geophysical technology, geophysical engineering, geophysical prospecting, and engineering geology also offer related training for beginning geologists.

Traditional geoscience courses emphasize classical geologic methods and concepts. Mineralogy, paleontology, stratigraphy, and structural geology are important courses for undergraduates. Students interested in environmental and regulatory fields should take courses in hydrology, hazardous waste management, environmental legislation, chemistry, fluid mechanics, and geologic logging.

In addition, students should take courses in related sciences, mathematics, English composition, and computer science. Students seeking graduate degrees in geology should concentrate on advanced courses in geology, placing major emphasis on their particular fields.

Certification or Licensing

The American Institute of Professional Geologists (AIPG) grants the certified professional geologist (CPG) designation to geologists who have earned a bachelor's degree or higher in the geological sciences and have eight years of professional experience (applicants with a master's degree need only seven years of professional experience and those with a Ph.D., five years). Candidates must also undergo peer review by three professional geologists (two of whom must be CPGs) and pay an application fee.

The institute also offers the member designation to geologists who are registered in various states and are not seeking AIPG certification. Applicants must have at least a bachelor's degree in the geological sciences with at least 36 semester hours of geology, be licensed by the state they wish to work in, undergo peer review, and pay an application fee. A student adjunct certification is also available to those who are majoring in the geological sciences.

More than 30 states require geologists to be registered or licensed. Most of these states require applicants (who have earned a bachelor's degree in the geological sciences) to pass the Fundamentals of Geology exam, a standardized written exam developed by the National Association of State Boards of Geology.

Other Requirements

In addition to academic training and work experience, geologists who work in the field or in administration must have skills in business administration and in working with other people. Computer modeling, data processing, and effective oral and written communication skills are important, as is the ability to think independently and creatively. Physical stamina is needed for those involved in fieldwork.

EXPLORING

If this career sounds interesting, try to read as much as possible about geology and geologists. Your best chance for association with geologists and geological work is to join clubs or organizations concerned with such things as rock collecting. Amateur geological groups and local museums also offer opportunities for you to gain exposure to the field of geology.

EMPLOYERS

Approximately 33,600 geoscientists (including geologists) are employed in the United States. The majority of geologists are employed in private industry. Some work for oil and gas extraction and mining companies, primarily in exploration. The rest work for business services, environmental and geotechnical consulting firms, or are self-employed as consultants to industry and government. The federal government employs geologists in the Department of the Interior (in the U.S. Geological Survey and the Bureau of Reclamation) and in the Departments of Defense, Agriculture, and Commerce. Geologists also work for state agencies, nonprofit research organizations, and museums. Many geologists hold faculty positions at colleges and universities and most of these combine their teaching with research.

STARTING OUT

After completing sufficient educational requirements, preferably a master's degree or doctorate, the geologist may look for work in various areas, including private industry and government. For those who wish to teach at the college level, a doctorate is required. College graduates may also take government civil service examinations or possibly find work on state geological surveys, which are sometimes based on civil service competition.

Geologists often begin their careers in field exploration or as research assistants in laboratories. As they gain experience, they are given more difficult assignments and may be promoted to supervisory positions, such as project leader or program manager.

ADVANCEMENT

A geologist with a bachelor's degree has little chance of advancing to higher-level positions. Continued formal training and work experience are necessary, especially as competition for these positions grows more intense. A doctorate is essential for most college or university teaching positions and is preferred for much research work.

EARNINGS

The U.S. Department of Labor reports that the median annual salary for geoscientists was $82,500 in 2010; the top paid 10 percent earned more than $160,910 while the lowest paid 10 percent earned less than $43,820 a year. In the federal government, the average salary for geologists in managerial, supervisory, and nonsupervisory positions was $94,560 a year. Those employed in the oil and gas extraction industries earned $136,270.

Although the petroleum, mineral, and mining industries offer higher salaries, competition for these jobs is stiff and there is less job security than in other areas. In addition, college and university teachers can earn additional income through research, writing, and consulting. Salaries for foreign assignments may be significantly higher than those in the United States.

Benefits for full-time workers include vacation and sick time, health, and sometimes dental, insurance, and pension or 401(k) plans. Self-employed geologists must provide their own benefits.

WORK ENVIRONMENT

Some geologists spend most of their time in a laboratory or office, working a regular 40-hour week in pleasant conditions; others divide their time between fieldwork and office or laboratory work. Those who work in the field often travel to remote sites by helicopter or four-wheel drive vehicle and cover large areas on foot. They may camp for extended periods of time in primitive conditions with the members of the geological team as their only companions. Exploration geologists often work overseas or in remote areas, and job relocation is not unusual. Marine geologists may spend considerable time at sea.

OUTLOOK

Employment of geologists is expected to grow faster than the average for all occupations through 2018, according to the *Occupational Outlook Handbook*. Opportunities in the field will be good because a large number of geologists are expected to retire during the next decade and demand for energy resources is expected to increase. Job opportunities will be especially strong for those with a master's degree who are familiar with computer modeling and the global positioning system (GPS). Geologists who are able to speak a foreign language and who are willing to work overseas will also have strong employment prospects. In addition to the oil and gas industries, geologists will be able to find jobs in environmental monitoring, protection, and reclamation.

FOR MORE INFORMATION

Visit the association's Web site for information on careers and membership for college students, as well as answers to frequently asked questions about the field.

American Association of Petroleum Geologists
PO Box 979
Tulsa, OK 74110-0979
Tel: 800-364-2274
http://www.aapg.org

For information on geoscience careers, contact
American Geological Institute
4220 King Street
Alexandria, VA 22302-1502
Tel: 703-379-2480
http://www.agiweb.org

For information on careers and certification, contact
American Institute of Professional Geologists
12000 North Washington Street, Suite 285
Thornton, CO 80241-3134
Tel: 303-412-6205
E-mail: aipg@aipg.org
http://www.aipg.org

*For career information and profiles of women in geophysics, visit
the AWG Web site.*
Association for Women Geoscientists (AWG)
12000 North Washington Street, Suite 285
Thornton, CO 80241-3134
Tel: 303-412-6219
E-mail: office@awg.org
http://www.awg.org

*For information on the position of state geologist and statistics on
minerals, groundwater, and other topics, contact*
Association of American State Geologists
http://www.stategeologists.org

For career information, contact
Association of Environmental and Engineering Geologists
PO Box 460518
Denver, CO 80246-0518
Tel: 303-757-2926
E-mail: aeg@aegweb.org
http://www.aegweb.org

For career information and job listings, contact
Geological Society of America
PO Box 9140
Boulder, CO 80301-9140
Tel: 888-443-4472
E-mail: gsaservice@geosociety.org
http://www.geosociety.org

For career information, contact
National Association of Black Geologists and Geophysicists
4212 San Felipe, Suite 420
Houston, TX 77027-2902
E-mail: nabgg_us@hotmail.com
http://www.nabgg.com

For information on the Fundamentals of Geology exam, contact
National Association of State Boards of Geology
PO Box 11591
Columbia, SC 29211-1591
Tel: 803-739-5676
http://www.asbog.org

For information about sedimentary geology and related disciplines, contact
Society for Sedimentary Geology
4111 South Darlington, Suite 100
Tulsa, OK 74135-6373
Tel: 800-865-9765
http://www.sepm.org

For information about economic geology, contact
Society of Economic Geologists
7811 Shaffer Parkway
Littleton, CO 80127-3732
Tel: 720-981-7882
E-mail: seg@segweb.org
http://www.segweb.org

For information on career opportunities, contact
U.S. Geological Survey
12201 Sunrise Valley Drive
Reston, VA 20192-0002
Tel: 888-275-8747
http://education.usgs.gov

For *information on geotechnical engineering, contact*
GEOENGINEER
http://www.geoengineer.org

INTERVIEW

Dr. Tony Runkel is the chief geologist for the Minnesota Geological Survey. He discussed his career with the editors of Careers in Focus: Geology.

Q. What made you want to become a geologist?

A. As early as third grade, I had a keen interest in rocks and fossils. Therefore there may have been some innate interest in the subject. Later, in college, an introductory geology class rekindled this interest, and, combined with a desire to have a job that included working outdoors, I decided that geology might be a great career.

Q. What is one thing that young people may not know about a career in geology?

A. Most people are unaware of the diversity of jobs in the field of geology, outside of academic research such as the study of dinosaurs. At best, some young people might know that geologists have a role in finding precious metals, such as gold, or in the exploration for oil and natural gas. But practicing geologists are involved with many other disciplines, including environmental-related research. Geologists play a key role in managing groundwater resources, and they play an important role in the engineering of large construction projects and in the evaluation of geologic hazards such as earthquakes, landslides, and floods.

Q. What are your main duties as chief geologist of the Minnesota Geological Survey?

A. My specific duty as chief geologist is to ensure that the geologic information we disseminate to the public is of high quality. As in any scientific field this includes careful evaluation of the products we produce, such as the geologic maps and reports that are used by the public. But much more of my time involves research focused on understanding how groundwater moves through the aquifers that supply the citizens of Minnesota with their drinking water.

Q. What are the most important personal and professional qualities for geologists?

A. I believe that the best geologists are those who have a strong passion for their career, combined with strong ethics.

Q. What are some of the pros and cons of your job?

A. By far the largest positive is that I am doing a job that I remain passionate about. It is challenging, interesting, and on top of that, the work we do benefits the people of Minnesota. The only con that comes to mind is that I am not conducting research outdoors nearly so much as I'd prefer.

Q. What is the employment outlook for geologists?

A. Right now I think the employment outlook is moderately good. Demand for geologists can be quite cyclic, but employment opportunities in the oil and gas industry, and mining, are fairly good. My understanding is that long-term projections indicate that demand for geologists will exceed newly graduated students, especially in environmental-related fields.

Geophysicists

OVERVIEW

Geophysicists are concerned with matter and energy and how they interact. They study the physical properties and structure of the earth, from its interior to its upper atmosphere, including land surfaces, subsurfaces, and bodies of water. There are approximately 33,600 geoscientists employed in the United States.

HISTORY

Geophysics is an important field that combines the sciences of geology and physics. Geology is the study of the history and composition of the earth as recorded by rock formations and fossils. Physics deals with all forms of energy, the properties of matter, and the relationship between energy and matter. The geophysicist is an "earth physicist," one who works with the physical aspects of the earth from its inner core to outer space.

This alliance between the earth and physical sciences is part of the progress that science has made in searching for new understandings of the world. Like the fields of biochemistry, biomathematics, space medicine, and nuclear physics, geophysics combines the knowledge of two disciplines. However, the importance of geophysics goes well beyond abstract theory. Geophysicists apply their knowledge to such practical problems as predicting earthquakes and tsunamis, locating raw materials and sources of power, and evaluating sites for power plants.

THE JOB

Geophysicists use the principles and techniques of geology, physics, chemistry, mathematics, and engineering to perform tests and

A geophysicist studies recordings of earthquake activity on seismic drums. *(Riccardo De Luca, AP Photo)*

conduct research on the surface, atmosphere, waters, and solid bodies of the earth. They study seismic, gravitational, electrical, thermal, and magnetic phenomena to determine the structure and composition of the earth, as well as the forces causing movement and warping of the surface.

Many geophysicists are involved in fieldwork, where they engage in exploration and prospecting. Others work in laboratories, where research activities are the main focus. They use computer-modeling software to develop and test their hypotheses. Photogrammetry, geographic information systems (GIS), and remote sensing technology is often used to gather geophysical data. In general, their instruments are highly complex and designed to take very precise measurements. Most geophysicists specialize in one of the following areas.

Geodesists measure the shape and size of the earth to determine fixed points, positions, and elevations on or near the earth's surface. Using the gravimeter, they perform surveys to measure minute variations in the earth's gravitational field. They also collect data that is useful in learning more about the weight, size, and mass of the earth. Geodesists are active in tracking satellites orbiting in outer space.

Geomagnetists use the magnetometer to measure variations in the earth's magnetic field from magnetic observatories and stations. They are also concerned with conditions affecting radio signals, solar phenomena, and many other aspects of space exploration. The data gathered can be most helpful in working with problems in radio and television transmission, telegraphy, navigation, mapping, and space exploration and space science.

Applied geophysicists use data gathered from the air, ground, and ocean floor, as well as computers, to analyze the earth's crust. They look for oil and mineral deposits and try to find sites for the safe disposal of hazardous wastes.

Exploration geophysicists, sometimes called *geophysical prospectors*, use seismic techniques to look for possible oil and gas deposits on land and in oceans. They may use sonar equipment to send sound waves deep into the earth or beneath the ocean surface. The resulting echo helps them estimate if an oil deposit lies hidden in the area.

Hydrologists are concerned with the surface and underground waters in the land areas of the earth. They map and chart the flow and the disposition of sediments, measure changes in water volume, and collect data on the form and intensity of precipitation, as well as on the disposition of water through evaporation and ground absorption. The information that the hydrologist collects is applied to problems in flood control, crop production, soil and water conservation, irrigation, and inland water projects. Some hydrologists study glaciers and their sedimentation.

Marine geophysicists are geophysicists who apply their training to the study of our world's oceans. They conduct research on how matter and energy affect the ocean. In particular, they study the makeup of the earth's surface and waters and how geophysical phenomena such as earthquakes, tsunamis, and underwater volcanoes and hydrothermal systems change them.

Seismologists use sound waves to study the earth's interior structure. They specialize in the study of earthquakes. With the aid of the seismogram and other instruments that record the location of earthquakes and the vibrations they cause, seismologists examine active fault lines and areas where earthquakes have occurred. They are often members of field teams whose purpose is to examine and evaluate possible building or construction sites. They also may explore for oil and minerals. In recent years, seismologists have contributed to the selection of missile launching sites. Seismologists who study the ocean floor can pinpoint areas where earthquakes may occur. Earthquakes can sometimes cause tsunamis, which can kill or injure people in regions far from the earthquake site. Seismologists also try to answer questions such as: What does the deep interior of the earth look like?, and What is the role of upper earth mantle structures in tectonic plate interactions?

Tectonophysicists study the structure of mountains and ocean basins, the properties of the earth's crust, and the physical forces and processes that cause movements and changes in the structure of the earth. A great deal of their work is research, and their findings are helpful in locating oil and mineral deposits.

Volcanologists study volcanoes, their location, and their activity. They are concerned with their origins and the phenomena of their processes.

Planetologists use data from artificial satellites and astronauts' equipment to study the makeup and atmosphere of the planets, the moon, and other bodies in our solar system. Recent advances in this field have greatly increased our knowledge of Jupiter, Saturn, and their satellites.

REQUIREMENTS

High School
A strong interest in the physical and earth sciences is essential for this field. You should take basic courses in earth science, physics, chemistry, and at least four years of mathematics. Advanced placement work in any of the mathematics and sciences is also helpful. Other recommended courses include mechanical drawing, shop, social studies, English, and computer science.

Postsecondary Training
A bachelor's degree in geophysics is required for most entry-level positions. Physics, mathematics, and chemistry majors can locate positions in geophysics, but some work in geology is highly desirable and often required, especially for certain government positions.

Graduate work at the master's or doctoral level is required for research, college teaching, and positions of a policy-making or policy-interpreting nature in private or government employment.

Many colleges and universities offer a bachelor's degree in geophysics, and a growing number of these institutions also award advanced degrees. An undergraduate major in geophysics is not usually required for entrance into a graduate program.

Other Requirements
If you seek employment in the federal government you will have to take a civil service examination and be able to meet other specified requirements.

You should also possess a strong aptitude in mathematics and science, particularly the physical and earth sciences, and an interest in observing nature, performing experiments, and studying the physical environment. Because geophysicists frequently spend time outdoors, you should enjoy outdoor activities such as hiking and camping.

EXPLORING

You can explore various aspects of this field by taking earth and physical science courses. Units of study dealing with electricity, rocks and minerals, metals and metallurgy, the universe and space, and weather and climate may offer you an opportunity for further learning about the field. Hobbies that deal with radio, electronics, and rock or map collecting also offer opportunities to learn about the basic principles involved in geophysics.

Some colleges and universities have a student chapter of the Society of Exploration Geophysicists that you can join. Employment as an aide or helper with a geophysical field party may be available during the summer months and provide you with the opportunity to study the physical environment and interact with geophysicists.

EMPLOYERS

Approximately 33,600 geoscientists (including geophysicists) are employed in the United States. Geophysicists are employed primarily by the petroleum industry, mining companies, exploration and consulting firms, and research institutions. A few geophysicists work as consultants, offering their services on a fee or contract basis. Many work for the federal government, mainly the National Geodetic Survey, the U.S. Geological Survey, and the Naval Oceanographic Office. Other geophysicists pursue teaching careers.

STARTING OUT

Most college career services offices are prepared to help students locate positions in business, industry, and government agencies. Other job contacts can be made through professors, friends, and relatives. Some companies visit college campuses in the spring of each year to interview candidates who are interested in positions as geophysicists. College career services offices can usually provide helpful information on job opportunities in the field of geophysics.

Additionally, some associations, such as the Seismological Society of America, offer job listings at their Web sites.

ADVANCEMENT

If employed by a private firm, a new employee with only a bachelor's degree will probably have an on-the-job training period. As a company trainee, the beginning geophysicist may be assigned to a number of different jobs. On a field party, the trainee will probably work with a junior geophysicist, which in many companies is the level of assignment received after the training has ended.

From a junior geophysicist, advancement is usually to intermediate geophysicist, and eventually to geophysicist. From this point, one can transfer to research positions or, if the geophysicist remains in fieldwork, to *party chief.*

The party chief coordinates the work of people in a crew, including trainees; junior, intermediate, and full geophysicists; surveyors; observers; drillers; shooters; and aides. Advancement with the company may eventually lead to supervisory and management positions.

Geophysicists can often transfer to other jobs in the fields of geology, physics, and engineering, depending on their qualifications and experience.

EARNINGS

The salaries of geophysicists are comparable to the earnings of those in other scientific professions. According to the U.S. Department of Labor, geoscientists (which includes geologists, geophysicists, and oceanographers) earned an average annual salary of $82,500 in 2010. The lowest paid 10 percent earned less than $43,820 per year, while the highest paid 10 percent earned more than $160,910 annually. In 2010, the average salary for a geophysicist working for the federal government was $95,580. Positions in colleges and universities offer annual salaries ranging from about $43,000 for instructors to $133,000 for full professors. Salaries depend upon experience, education, and professional rank. Faculty members may teach in summer school for additional compensation and also engage in writing, consulting, and research for government, industry, or business.

Additional compensation is awarded to geophysicists who are required to live outside the United States.

Both the federal government and private industry provide additional benefits, including vacations, retirement pensions, health and life insurance, and sick leave benefits.

WORK ENVIRONMENT

Geophysicists employed in laboratories or offices generally work a regular 40-hour week under typical office conditions. Field geophysicists work under a variety of conditions and often the hours are irregular. They are outdoors much of the time in all kinds of weather. The work requires carrying small tools and equipment and occasionally some heavy lifting. The field geophysicist is often required to travel and work in isolated areas. Volcanologists, for example, may face dangerous conditions when visiting and gathering data near an erupting volcano.

OUTLOOK

Employment of geophysicists is expected to grow faster than the average for all occupations through 2018, according to the *Occupational Outlook Handbook*. The total number of graduates with degrees in the geophysical sciences is expected to remain small and insufficient to meet the moderate increase in industry job openings. Those with advanced degrees, experience in the field, and a willingness to travel will have the best employment opportunities.

The petroleum industry, the largest employer of geophysicists, has increased its exploration activities, and more geophysicists will be needed to locate less-accessible fuel and mineral deposits and to do research on such problems as radioactivity, cosmic and solar radiation, and the use of geothermal energy to generate electricity. The petroleum industry is also expected to expand operations overseas, which may create new jobs for those who are willing to travel.

More geophysicists will be needed to study water conservation and flood control and to assist in space science projects. The growing need to find new sources of energy will undoubtedly make the work of geophysicists more important and more challenging during the next few decades.

FOR MORE INFORMATION

For information on geoscience careers, contact
American Geological Institute
4220 King Street
Alexandria, VA 22302-1502

Tel: 703-379-2480
http://www.agiweb.org

For information on local meetings, publications, job opportunities, and science news, contact
American Geophysical Union
2000 Florida Avenue, NW
Washington, DC 20009-1277
Tel: 800-966-2481
http://www.agu.org

For career information and profiles of women in geophysics, visit the AWG Web site.
Association for Women Geoscientists (AWG)
12000 North Washington Street, Suite 285
Thornton, CO 80241-3134
Tel: 303-412-6219
E-mail: office@awg.org
http://www.awg.org

For information on careers and the society's specialty divisions, contact
Geological Society of America
PO Box 9140
Boulder, CO 80301-9140
Tel: 888-443-4472
E-mail: gsaservice@geosociety.org
http://www.geosociety.org

For an overview of remote sensing, contact
Geoscience and Remote Sensing Society
Institute of Electrical and Electronics Engineers
445 Hoes Lane
Piscataway, NJ 08854-4141
E-mail: info@ieee-grss.org
http://www.grss-ieee.org

For career information, contact
National Association of Black Geologists and Geophysicists
4212 San Felipe, Suite 420
Houston, TX 77027-2902
E-mail: nabgg_us @ hotmail.com
http://www.nabgg.com

For information about marine geophysics and oceanography, contact
National Oceanic and Atmospheric Administration
c/o U.S. Department of Commerce
1401 Constitution Avenue, NW, Room 5128
Washington, DC 20230-0001
http://www.noaa.gov

For career information and job listings, contact
Seismological Society of America
201 Plaza Professional Building
El Cerrito, CA 94530-4003
Tel: 510-525-5474
E-mail: info@seismosoc.org
http://www.seismosoc.org

For information on careers in geophysics and a virtual museum, visit the society's Web site.
Society of Exploration Geophysicists
PO Box 702740
Tulsa, OK 74170-2740
Tel: 918-497-5500
E-mail: membership@seg.org
http://www.seg.org

To read the online publication Become a Geophysicist . . . A What?, *visit*
U.S. Geological Survey
http://education.usgs.gov or http://earthquake.usgs.gov/learn/
    kids/become.php

To learn more about coastal and marine geology, visit
U.S. Geological Survey: Coastal and Marine Geology Program
http://marine.usgs.gov

Groundwater Professionals

OVERVIEW

Groundwater professionals are different types of scientists and engineers concerned with water supplies beneath the earth's surface. For example, they search for new water sources and ensure safe water supplies.

HISTORY

In addition to the water that can be seen on the surface of the earth, such as lakes, streams, rivers, ponds, canals, and oceans, there is water under the ground, known as groundwater. Groundwater includes things like underground streams and aquifers, which are layers of water-bearing porous rock or sediment. People have been tapping into various groundwater sources for centuries, using the water for everything from drinking to irrigation.

Artesian wells, for example, are used to provide water (including drinking water) in some parts of the world. They are created by boring down into aquifers; the resulting pressure causes water in the aquifer to rise up in the well. Australia has the world's biggest artesian well system; in the United States, artesian systems supply water to parts of the Great Plains and the East Coast.

Like other natural resources, groundwater has been the focus of increasing attention in the United States since the 1970s. The U.S. government has recognized threats to this vital supply of water and passed laws to protect it. At first, people in the field and in related fields were called on to adapt their skills to meeting the new

School Subjects
Earth science
Mathematics

Personal Skills
Communication/ideas
Technical/scientific

Work Environment
Indoors and outdoors
Primarily one location

Minimum Education Level
Bachelor's degree

Salary Range
$48,280 to $75,690 to
$112,490+

Certification or Licensing
Voluntary

Outlook
Faster than the average

DOT
024

GOE
02.02.01

NOC
2212

O*NET-SOC
19-2043.00

regulations. In recent years, especially as the regulations have gotten more technical and complex, demand for people who specialize in groundwater science has risen dramatically.

A look at the groundwater situation in one state, Florida, demonstrates some of the potential problems. The groundwater in many areas is located not very far under the surface—just a few feet, in some cases. A surging population is drawing heavily on these supplies, threatening to use them faster than they can replenish themselves. Rapid development (farming, mining, construction, industry) offers high potential for disrupting the vulnerable groundwater.

Also, in some cases, below the aquifers in Florida that carry good water are aquifers that carry poor-quality water, high in sulfates. Drawing down too far into the aquifers that have good water might accidentally pull up the bad water from the aquifer below it, or, worse, pull over saltwater from the coast. Once saltwater gets in, that aquifer is probably lost as a source of drinking water.

Another groundwater hazard is the possibility of a fuel, chemical, or other spill on the ground. Hazardous chemicals in these substances can soak through the soil and reach the groundwater, contaminating it. Even good-quality groundwater usually is treated before it is used (although in some places, like outlying rural areas, people drink untreated groundwater, drawing it right out of the ground). Regular water treatment facilities are not designed to handle removal of hazardous substances. That requires special steps, is usually more difficult and expensive than cleaning surface water, and sometimes does not work.

This is, in fact, a national concern. Today, according to the National Ground Water Association, some 44 percent of the United States relies on groundwater for its drinking water. At the same time, better methods for detecting contaminants have revealed that contamination of groundwater is more extensive than was previously known.

Legislation (including the Resource Conservation and Recovery Act; the Comprehensive Environmental Response, Compensation, and Liability Act; the Superfund Amendments and Reauthorization Act; and the Safe Drinking Water Act) mandates the cleanup, monitoring, and protection of the nation's groundwater supplies. This direction was strengthened by later amendments to such laws. Recent stricter regulations applying to landfills, for example, acknowledge the potential risks of these operations to groundwater. In particular, seepage from landfills can get into the groundwater and contaminate it. New landfills must have double liners and other features to help prevent seepage; existing landfills have new rules about closing and

Did You Know?

- Groundwater makes up an estimated 30.1 percent of the world's freshwater. It is estimated that 26 percent of the freshwater used in the United States comes from groundwater.
- Approximately 44 million Americans depend on private groundwater wells for their water supply. Another 90 million Americans rely on public groundwater systems for their water needs.
- People can only live about five to seven days without water.
- More than 1.1 billion people worldwide do not have access to a safe and adequate water supply.

Sources: National Ground Water Association, Association of American State Geologists, WaterPartners International

capping the landfill to try to stop or minimize seepage. Groundwater monitoring equipment is used to take constant readings of the area's groundwater and determine if any seepage is occurring.

The special problems of groundwater, people's reliance on it, and the laws passed to protect it all have contributed to the growing need for groundwater professionals. Groundwater work is part of the water quality management segment of the environmental industry, which accounts for about one-quarter of all spending on the environment.

THE JOB

No one really has the title groundwater professional; instead, it describes any of a number of different positions within the groundwater industry. These include different types of scientists, engineers, and technicians employed in government, private industry, and nonprofit organizations at various tasks designed to ensure safe, effective, and lawful use of groundwater supplies. In earlier times, geologists were often called upon to do groundwater work, and they continue to be important players in the field today. Geology is the science of the earth's history, composition, and structure. Specialties in the groundwater field today include hydrogeology and hydrology. *Hydrogeologists* study the science of groundwater supplies. *Hydrologists* study underground and surface water and its properties, including how water is distributed and how it moves through land. Other professionals in the groundwater industry include chemists, geological engineers, water quality technicians, computer modelers, environmental engineers, chemists, bioremediation specialists, petroleum geologists, and mining engineers.

Employers of groundwater professionals include local water districts, government agencies, consulting firms, landfill operations, private industry, and others with a stake in successful groundwater management. What groundwater professionals do depends on the employer.

For example, local or regional authorities usually are responsible for ensuring a safe and adequate water supply for people in the area. For example, any time people want to make a new use of water or do something that might affect water in the area (like building a road, drilling a well, or laying a sewer), they have to get a permit. Before it will issue a permit, the authority has groundwater professionals check the site and decide if the use is safe. Typically, geologists do the necessary fieldwork, while engineers handle the actual obtaining of permits.

For a local or regional authority, groundwater professionals might help locate new sources of water in the area, which typically involves surveying the area, drilling for samples, and measuring the capacity of any water reserves found. They find the source of the groundwater and determine its ability to replenish itself if tapped for use, decide how the water would best be used, and make a recommendation to the authority. If the authority approves, a new well system is designed to tap the groundwater, and wells are drilled.

States are big employers of groundwater professionals. What groundwater professionals do for a state depends greatly on what part of the country it is in. The mapping of known groundwater supplies, often using computer modeling to show groundwater flow and possible effects of contamination, is often part of their efforts.

For both state and local or regional authorities, combating the effects of contamination is a critical task. The nature and extent of contamination, combined with the geologic and hydrologic characteristics of the surrounding land, determine whether the water supply is permanently tainted or can be made usable again in the future. Groundwater professionals design systems to reduce or stop contamination.

Another big employer is consulting firms. Regulations for waste treatment and disposal are becoming more and more strict, and that means that more technical expertise is required. Lacking that expertise themselves, many waste generators in the public and private sectors turn to consulting firms for help. Consultants may be

Hydrologists adjust instruments that will monitor glacier movement and thinning. *(David J. Sheakley, AP Photo)*

called in to help with a hazardous waste cleanup around a landfill, at a Superfund site (an abandoned hazardous waste site), or at another cleanup, or they may help a private industrial company devise a system to handle its waste. Groundwater professionals can be very useful to such consulting firms. For example, if a landfill is leaking waste into a source of groundwater, a groundwater specialist could devise solutions, such as digging new drainage systems for the landfill or building new containment facilities. A groundwater professional with a consulting firm might work close to home or travel to job sites around the country or even around the world.

REQUIREMENTS

High School
At the high school level, you can prepare for a career in groundwater work by taking a lot of science and math. Technology is important in this field, so make sure you have computer skills. Also, focus on developing your writing and speech skills. Reports, proposals, memos, scientific papers, and other forms of written and verbal

communication are likely to be part of your job as a groundwater professional.

Postsecondary Training
A bachelor's degree is the minimum requirement for being a professional in this field. Geology, civil engineering, and chemistry are the most common undergraduate degrees in this field today. Other appropriate majors are engineering, geology, hydrogeology, geophysics, petroleum geology, mining engineering, and other related degrees. Another possibility is a degree in hydrology, although it is not currently offered by many schools. Appropriate course work at the undergraduate level includes chemistry, physics, calculus, groundwater geology, groundwater hydrology, engineering hydrology, and fluid mechanics. It is also a good idea to learn how to do computer modeling, mapping, and related tasks. Undergraduate degrees are sufficient for getting a job doing activities such as on-site sampling and measurement.

A degree in hydrogeology is usually obtained at the master's level. This degree and some experience will place you among the most sought-after workers in the environmental industry.

Certification or Licensing
Some certification programs have been developed to measure experience and knowledge of groundwater science. Both the American Institute of Hydrology and the National Ground Water Association offer voluntary certification programs. Contact these organizations for more information.

Other Requirements
Patience, persistence, curiosity, attention to detail, and good analytic skills are all useful for a groundwater professional. You would be likely to work as part of a team and have people to answer to, whether a supervisor, the government, a client, or all three. You would also probably have to be familiar with many regulations, often complex ones.

EXPLORING
You should hold one or more internships while in college (check with your college career services office for opportunities). You also might be able to find a part-time or summer job with a consulting firm. In addition, check into research opportunities with your professors at

your school. You may be able to earn a small salary while gaining experience in fieldwork, compiling and interpreting data, or doing computer modeling. Volunteering at a nonprofit environmental organization might also be an option. Finally, you can also learn more about groundwater by visiting the Virtual Museum of Ground Water History online at http://info.ngwa.org/museum/museum.cfm.

EMPLOYERS

Employers of groundwater professionals include local water districts, government agencies, consulting firms, landfill operations, private industry, and others with a stake in successful groundwater management.

STARTING OUT

There are many ways to find openings in the industry. One obvious place to start is the want ads, in the daily newspaper, online, and in various professional journals. Local chapters of groundwater and geological societies sometimes have lists of job opportunities or bulletin boards with important notices. New graduates can also look for work at state employment offices, local or regional water authorities, or the local branches of federal agencies.

ADVANCEMENT

Those starting out with undergraduate degrees are likely to do tasks like sampling and measuring work. What an employee needs to advance will depend on the employer but probably will include some years of experience plus an advanced degree. It is advisable to keep up on the latest developments in the field through seminars, workshops, and other courses.

Advancement in private consulting firms will likely include promotion to an administrative position, which will mean spending more time in the office, dealing with clients, and directing the activities of other groundwater specialists and office staff. Those working for a local, regional, state, or federal organization may rise to an administrative level, meeting with planning commissions, public interest groups, legislative bodies, and industry groups.

Another option is for groundwater professionals to strike out on their own. With some experience, for example, ambitious professionals might start their own consulting firm.

EARNINGS

Earnings for groundwater professionals vary greatly depending on the type of work they do, training and experience required for the work, geographic region, type of employer, and other factors. Groundwater professionals earn salaries in the upper range of those for all water industry professionals. The U.S. Department of Labor (DOL) reports that median annual earnings of hydrologists were $75,690 in 2010. The lowest paid 10 percent earned less than $48,280, and the highest paid 10 percent earned $112,490 or more.

Benefits depend on the employer. They might include paid vacation, sick days, personal days, health and dental insurance, tuition reimbursement, retirement savings plans, and use of company vehicles.

WORK ENVIRONMENT

Fieldwork might mean going to natural areas to survey the geophysical characteristics of a site. Groundwater professionals may need to take water samples from the monitoring wells near a gas station, fuel storage facility, landfill, sewage treatment plant, or manufacturing company. They may oversee the digging of a new well system or check to see how a new well system is running. Although responsibilities depend on a professional's specific job, some work outside the office and outdoors is frequently part of the job.

In addition to fieldwork, groundwater professionals spend time working in offices. Some professionals, in fact, may spend most or all of their time indoors. Conditions in offices vary by employer, but offices are generally equipped with state-of-the-art technology. Most groundwater professionals work a 40-hour week, depending on project deadlines or unexpected developments in the field.

OUTLOOK

The field of groundwater science remains a promising career choice for motivated, intelligent students. The *Occupational Outlook Handbook* predicts that employment for hydrologists will grow faster than the average for all occupations through 2018. Employment for environmental scientists will grow much faster than the average during this same time span. The continued growth of our nation's population makes finding and remediating groundwater supplies an even more pressing issue in the 21st century. Private industry must continue to comply with government regulations, including those related to keeping groundwater safe from contamination. Local, regional, and state authorities need to map, develop, and protect their groundwater supplies. Consultants need the specific expertise that groundwater professionals can offer, for clients both in the United States and abroad. Research is needed to develop new ways to treat contaminated groundwater, to prevent spills or leaks, and to develop systems that will make the most of groundwater supplies. All of this means work for groundwater professionals for the near future. Private-sector consulting firms should offer the best employment prospects. Groundwater professionals who have an understanding of both the scientific and engineering aspects of waste remediation will have especially promising career opportunities, according to the DOL.

FOR MORE INFORMATION

For the brochure Careers in the Geosciences *and listings of geoscience departments, visit the institute's Web site.*
American Geological Institute
4220 King Street
Alexandria, VA 22302-1502
Tel: 703-379-2480
http://www.agiweb.org

For information on the hydrologic sciences, contact
American Geophysical Union
2000 Florida Avenue, NW
Washington, DC 20009-1277
Tel: 800-966-2481
http://www.agu.org

For information on certification, college student chapters, and related organizations, contact
American Institute of Hydrology
Southern Illinois University-Carbondale
Engineering D, Mail Code 6603, 1230 Lincoln Drive
Carbondale, IL 62901-4336
Tel: 618-453-7809
E-mail: aih@engr.siu.edu
http://www.aihydrology.org

For information on water quality and supply, contact
American Water Works Association
6666 West Quincy Avenue
Denver, CO 80235-3098

Tel: 800-926-7337
http://www.awwa.org

For information on grants, internships, and issues in geoscience, contact
Geological Society of America
PO Box 9140
Boulder, CO 80301-9140
Tel: 888-443-4472
E-mail: gsaservice@geosociety.org
http://www.geosociety.org
http://gsahydro.fiu.edu

For information on certification, contact
National Ground Water Association
601 Dempsey Road
Westerville, OH 43081-8978
Tel: 800-551-7379
E-mail: ngwa@ngwa.org
http://www.ngwa.org

For general information about groundwater, visit the following Web sites:
U.S. Environmental Protection Agency
Office of Ground Water and Drinking Water (4601)
Ariel Rios Building
1200 Pennsylvania Avenue, NW
Washington, DC 20460-0003
http://water.epa.gov/drink

U.S. Geological Survey
Water Resources Division
12201 Sunrise Valley Drive
Reston, VA 20192-0002
Tel: 888-275-8747
http://water.usgs.gov/ogw

Laboratory Testing Technicians

OVERVIEW

Laboratory testing technicians who work in geology conduct tests on rocks, minerals, soil, and water. Their laboratory duties include measuring and evaluating materials, recording data, and maintaining and ordering supplies. Some technicians may be required to collect samples in the field.

HISTORY

In the early days of geology, geoscientists conducted their own testing of soils, minerals, and other compounds. As technological breakthroughs increased the type of testing methods available, demand developed for specially trained professionals who could test compounds under precise scientific conditions. Today, geological laboratory testing technicians play an important role in analyzing soil, rocks, minerals, water, and other elements found at sites—freeing geologists up for more advanced scientific study and research.

THE JOB

Laboratory testing technicians assist geologists and other scientists in conducting tests on rocks, minerals, soil, water, and other substances. For example, some laboratory testing technicians test shale, sand, and other earthen materials to find their petroleum and/or mineral content. Tests are run on core samples during oil well drilling to determine what's present in the well bore. Technicians who specialize in testing

Learn More About It

McGraw-Hill. *Dictionary of Geology & Mineralogy.* 2d ed. New York: McGraw-Hill Professional, 2003.
Mitchell, James R. *The Rockhound's Handbook.* 2d ed. Baldwin Park, Calif.: Gem Guides Book Company, 2008.
Pellant, Chris. *Smithsonian Handbooks: Rocks & Minerals.* New York: DK ADULT, 2002.
Polk, Patti. *Collecting Rocks, Gems & Minerals: Easy Identification, Values, Lapidary Uses.* Cincinnati, Ohio: Krause Publications, 2010.
Ward, David. *Fossils.* Rev. ed. New York: DK ADULT, 2002.

ores and minerals for metal content are called *assayers*. Other technicians might conduct tests on soil samples taken near the site of a chemical spill to ensure that the chemicals have not leached into the earth and are contaminating the local food or water supply.

Some basic equipment used by laboratory testing technicians includes strainers and geological screens, brushes, plastic and glass vials, tweezers, dental picks, eyedroppers, magnifying glasses, beakers, magnets, scales, calipers, and microscopes.

Regardless of the specific nature of the tests conducted by technicians, they must always keep detailed records of every step. Laboratory technicians often do a great deal of writing and must make charts, graphs, and other displays to illustrate results. They may be called on to interpret test results, to draw overall conclusions, and to make recommendations. Laboratory testing technicians must be comfortable using computer software programs such as Microsoft Word, Access, and Excel and computer graphic programs. Some technicians have supervisory duties and manage small staffs of laboratory technicians. Occasionally, laboratory testing technicians travel to field sites to collect samples. Others appear as witnesses in court to provide testimony regarding their laboratory findings.

REQUIREMENTS

High School

If working as a laboratory testing technician sounds interesting to you, you can prepare for this work by taking at least two years of mathematics and at least a year each of chemistry, physics, and earth science in high school. You should also consider taking shop classes to become accustomed to working with tools and to develop manual dexterity. Classes in English and writing will provide you with good experience doing research and writing reports. Take computer science classes so that you become familiar with using this tool.

Postsecondary Training
A high school diploma is the minimum requirement for finding work as a laboratory testing technician. However, a two-year associate's degree in geology, minerals engineering, soil science, or a related field is highly recommended. Many community colleges or technical schools offer two-year degree programs in a specific technology. Completing the associate's degree will greatly enhance your resume, help you in finding full-time positions, and allow you to advance rapidly in your field.

Other Requirements
Laboratory technicians should be detail oriented and enjoy figuring out how things work. They should like problem solving and troubleshooting. Laboratory technicians must have the patience to repeat a test many times, perhaps even on the same compound. They must be able to follow directions carefully but also should be independent and motivated to work on their own until their assigned tasks are completed. Other important traits include good organizational and communication skills.

EXPLORING
Due to the precision and training required in the field, it is unlikely that as a high school student you will be able to find a part-time or summer job as a laboratory testing technician. However, you can explore the career by visiting the Web sites of college geology, soil science, or minerals engineering programs and try to arrange an information interview with a professor. Ask about the required classes, the opportunities available in your area, and any other questions you have. Although you probably won't be able to get work as a laboratory testing technician at this point, some research companies and government agencies do offer summer jobs to high school students to work in their offices or mail rooms. While these jobs do not offer hands-on technical experience, they do allow you to experience the work environment.

EMPLOYERS

Geological laboratory testing technicians are employed at private and government laboratories that are located all over the country. Major federal employers of geological laboratory testing technicians include the U.S. Geological Survey, the Minerals Management Service, the Bureau of Land Management, the National Oceanic and Atmospheric Administration, the U.S. Forest Service, and the Army Corps of Engineers. Other employers include museums, the energy industry, and colleges and universities.

STARTING OUT

Technical schools often help place graduating technicians. Many laboratories contact these schools directly looking for student employees or interns. Students can also contact local laboratories and government agencies at all levels to find out about job openings in their area. Technicians often begin as trainees who are supervised by more experienced workers. As they gain experience, technicians take on more responsibilities and are allowed to work more independently.

ADVANCEMENT

Skilled laboratory technicians may be promoted to manager or supervisor of a division in their company or agency. Experienced technicians may start their own testing laboratories or return to school to become engineers, physicists, soil scientists, or geologists.

EARNINGS

Earnings for laboratory testing technicians vary based on the type of work they do, their education and experience, and even the size of the laboratory and its location. The U.S. Department of Labor (DOL) reports that science technicians (a category that includes laboratory testing technicians) earned the following mean annual salaries by specialty in 2010: chemical technicians, $42,040; geological and petroleum technicians, $54,020; and environmental science and protection technicians, $41,380. Salaries for science technicians ranged from less than $28,000 to $96,000 or more.

Salaries increase as technicians gain experience and as they take on supervisory responsibility. Most organizations that employ laboratory testing technicians offer medical benefits, sick leave, and vacation time. However, these benefits will depend on the individual employer.

WORK ENVIRONMENT

Laboratory testing technicians typically work a 40-hour week. During especially busy times or in special circumstances, they may be required to work overtime. Most technicians work in clean, well-lighted laboratories where attention is paid to neatness and organization. Some laboratory testing technicians have their own offices, while others work in large single-room laboratories.

Some technicians may be required to go outside their laboratories to collect samples of materials for testing at locations, which can be hot, cold, wet, muddy, and uncomfortable. Occasionally, laboratory testing technicians may be asked to participate in field research. This will require them to be away from home for long periods of time and work closely—and efficiently—with an interdisciplinary team in close quarters.

OUTLOOK

Overall, employment for laboratory workers is expected to grow about as fast as the average for all careers through 2018, according to the DOL. Environmental concerns and dwindling natural resources are causing many manufacturers to look for better ways to develop ores, minerals, and other substances from the earth. Laboratory technicians will be needed to test new production procedures as well as prototypes of new products.

Some specialties may experience growth that is slightly slower than the average; for example, those who work with stone, clay, glass, and fabricated metal products may experience this slow growth. Little employment change is expected for geological technicians.

Technicians in any specialty who have strong educational backgrounds, keep up with developing technologies, and demonstrate knowledge of testing equipment and computer software and databases will have the best employment opportunities.

FOR MORE INFORMATION

The ACS provides career information and has information on new developments in the field.
American Chemical Society (ACS)
1155 16th Street, NW
Washington, DC 20036-4839
Tel: 800-227-5558
E-mail: help@acs.org
http://portal.acs.org/portal/acs/corg/content

This society offers membership for college students and provides industry news.

The Minerals, Metals, and Materials Society
184 Thorn Hill Road
Warrendale, PA 15086-7514
Tel: 800-759-4867
http://www.tms.org

For information on member laboratories, visit the association's Web site.

National Association of Marine Laboratories
http://www.naml.org

Mining Engineers

OVERVIEW

Mining engineers deal with the exploration, location, and planning for removal of minerals and mineral deposits from the earth. These include metals (iron, copper), nonmetallic minerals (limestone, gypsum), and coal. Mining engineers conduct preliminary surveys of mineral deposits and examine them to ascertain whether they can be extracted efficiently and economically, using either underground or surface mining methods. They plan and design the development of mine shafts and tunnels, devise means of extracting minerals, and select the methods to be used in transporting the minerals to the surface. They supervise all mining operations and are responsible for mine safety. Mining engineers normally specialize in design, research and development, or production. *Mining equipment engineers* may specialize in design, research, testing, or sales of equipment and services. Mines also require *safety engineers*.

There are approximately 7,100 mining and geological engineers employed in the United States.

HISTORY

The development of mining technology stretches back some 50,000 years to the period when people began digging pits and stripping surface cover in search of stone and flint for tools. Between 8000 and 3000 B.C., the search for quality flint led people to sink shafts and drive galleries into limestone deposits.

By about 1300 B.C., the Egyptians and other Near Eastern peoples were mining copper and gold by driving adits (near-horizontal entry tunnels) into hillsides, then sinking inclined shafts from which they drove extensive galleries. They supported the gallery roofs with pillars of uncut ore or wooden props.

Providing adequate ventilation posed a difficult problem in ancient underground mines. Because of the small dimensions of the passageways, air circulated poorly. All methods of ventilating the mines relied on the natural circulation of air by draft and convection. To assist this process, ancient engineers carefully calculated the number, location, and depth of the shafts. At the great Greek mining complex of Laurion, they sank shafts in pairs and drove parallel galleries from them with frequent crosscuts between galleries to assist airflow. Lighting a fire in one shaft caused a downdraft in the other.

Ancient Roman engineers made further advances in the mining techniques of the Greeks and Egyptians. They mined more ambitiously than the Greeks, sometimes exploiting as many as four levels by means of deep connecting shafts. Careful planning enabled them to drive complicated networks of exploratory galleries at various depths. Buckets of rock and ore could be hoisted up the main shaft by means of a windlass. Unlike the Greeks and Egyptians, the Romans often worked mines far below groundwater level. Engineers overcame the danger of flooding to some extent by developing effective, if expensive, drainage methods and machinery. Where terrain allowed, they devised an elaborate system of crosscuts to channel off the water. In addition, they adapted Archimedean screws—originally used for crop irrigation—to drain mine workings. A series of inclined screws, each emptying water into a tub emptied by a screw above it, could raise a considerable amount of water in a short time. It took only one man to rotate each screw, which made it perhaps the most efficient application of labor until engineers discovered the advantage of cutting halls large enough for an animal to rotate the screw. By the first century A.D., the Romans had designed water wheels, which greatly increased the height to which water could be raised in mines.

Mining engineering advanced little from Roman times until the 11th century. From this period on, however, basic mining operations such as drainage, ventilation, and hoisting underwent increasing mechanization. In his book *De Re Metallica* (1556), the German scholar Georgius Agricola presented a detailed description of the devices and practices mining engineers had developed since ancient times. Drainage pumps in particular grew more and more sophisticated. One pump sucked water from mines by the movement of water-wheel-driven pistons.

As mines went deeper, technological problems required new engineering solutions. During the 18th century, engineers developed

Facts About the U.S. Coal Mining Industry

• Coal is found in 38 states.
• The coal mining industry employs nearly 134,000 people.
• Fifty percent of U.S. electricity is generated from coal.
• It is estimated that the U.S. has nearly 265 billion tons of recoverable coal reserves.
• At our current usage rate, this is enough to last 235 more years.

Sources: Energy Information Institute, National Mining Association

cheap, reliable steam-powered pumps to raise water in mines. Steam-powered windlasses also came into use. In the 1800s, engineers invented power drills for making shot holes for rock-breaking explosives. This greatly increased the capability to mine hard rock. In coal mines, revolving-wheel cutters—powered by steam, then by compressed air, then by electricity—relieved miners from the dangerous task of undercutting coal seams by hand. As late as the mid-19th century, ore was still being pushed or hauled through mines by people and animals. After 1900, however, electric locomotives, conveyor belts, and large-capacity rubber-tired vehicles came into wide use so that haulage could keep pace with mechanized ore breaking. The development of large, powerful machines also made possible the removal of vast amounts of material from open-pit mines.

THE JOB

Before the decision is made to mine a newly discovered mineral deposit, mining engineers must go through successive stages of information gathering, evaluation, and planning. As long as they judge the project to be economically viable, they proceed to the next stage. Review and planning for a major mining project may take a decade or longer and may cost many millions of dollars.

First mining engineers try to get a general idea of the deposit's potential. They accomplish this by reviewing geological data, product marketing information, and government requirements for permits, public hearings, and environmental protection. Based on this review, they prepare rough cost estimates and economic analyses. If it appears possible to mine the deposit at a competitive price with an acceptable return on investment, mining engineers undertake a more detailed review.

Meanwhile, geologists continue to explore the mineral deposit in order to ascertain its dimensions and character. Once the deposit has been reasonably well defined, mining engineers estimate the percentage of the deposit that can be profitably extracted. This estimate, which takes into account the ore's grade (value) and tonnage (volume and density), constitutes the minable ore reserve. It provides mining engineers with enough specific information to refine their economic appraisal and justify further analysis.

At this stage, engineers begin the process of selecting the most suitable mining method—one that will yield the largest profit consistent with safety and efficient ore extraction. In considering the adaptability of mining methods to the deposit, they rely heavily on rock mechanics and geologic data. Measurements of the stresses, strains, and displacements in the rock surrounding the ore body help engineers predict roof-support requirements and settling of rock masses during excavation. Evaluation of the deposit's geologic features (such as the dimensions, inclination, strength, and physical character of the ore and overlying rock) enables engineers to place mine openings in stable rock, avoid underground water, and plan overall excavation procedures. If the evaluation calls for surface mining, engineers must decide where to dig the pits and where to put the rock and soil removed during mining.

Having estimated the ore reserve, chosen a mining method, and begun mine planning, engineers can determine daily (or yearly) mine output tonnage in light of product demand. They also select equipment and help plan and size the mine's plant, support, ore-processing, and shipping facilities.

For underground mining, mining engineers must determine the number and location of mine shafts, tunnels, and main extraction openings. They must also determine the size, number, kind, and layout of the various pieces of equipment. If the project continues to appear economically viable, construction begins.

As actual mine-making proceeds, mining engineers supervise operations. They train crews of workers and supervisors. The stress fields around the mine workings change as the mine expands. Engineers and engineering technicians must inspect the roof of underground cavities to ensure that it continues to have adequate support. Engineers must also continually monitor the quality of air in the mine to ensure proper ventilation. In addition, mining engineers inspect and repair mining equipment. Some mining engineers help plan ways of restoring or reclaiming the land around mine sites so that it can be used for other purposes. Some mining engineers specialize in designing equipment used to excavate and operate mines. This equipment typically includes ventilation systems, earth- and rock-moving conveyors, and underground railroads and elevators. Engineers also design the equipment that chips and cuts rock and coal. Others select and determine the placement of explosives used to blast ore deposits.

Mining engineers also work for firms that sell mining supplies and equipment. Experienced mining engineers teach in colleges and universities and serve as independent consultants to industry and government.

REQUIREMENTS

High School

To meet the standards set by most engineering colleges, high school students should take as much math and science as possible. Minimum course work includes elementary and intermediate algebra, plane geometry, trigonometry, chemistry, and physics. Courses in solid geometry, advanced algebra, and basic computer functions are highly recommended. In addition, many engineering colleges require three years of English (preferably emphasizing composition and public speaking) and social science (especially economics and history). Course work in foreign languages also is helpful, because many engineers work overseas.

Postsecondary Training

A bachelor's degree in engineering, preferably with a major in mining engineering, from an accredited engineering program is the minimum requirement for beginning mining engineering jobs. The organization that accredits engineering programs in the United States is the Accreditation Board for Engineering and Technology (ABET). ABET-accredited mining engineering programs assure students that their education will prepare them for professional practice and graduate study.

In a typical undergraduate engineering program, students spend the first two years studying basic sciences, such as mathematics, physics, and chemistry, as well as introductory engineering. Students must also study such subjects as economics, foreign languages, history, management, and writing. These courses equip students with skills they will need in their future work as engineers. The remaining years of college are devoted mostly to engineering courses, usually with a concentration in mining engineering. Engineering programs can last from four to six years. Those that require five to six years to complete may award a master's degree or provide a cooperative engineering education program. Cooperative programs allow students to combine classroom education and practical work experience with a participating mining company or engineering firm.

After completing their formal studies and landing a job, many mining engineers continue their education. They take courses, attend workshops, and read professional journals in order to keep up with developments in their field. Continuing education also enables them to acquire expertise in new technical areas. Some mining engineers pursue advanced degrees. A graduate degree is needed for most teaching and research positions and for many management positions. Some mining engineers pursue graduate study in engineering, business, or law.

Visit the Society for Mining, Metallurgy, and Exploration's Web site, http://www.smenet.org, for a list of postsecondary mining engineering programs.

Certification or Licensing

Regardless of their educational credentials, mining engineers normally must obtain professional certification in the states in which they work. Professional registration is mandatory for mining engineers whose work may affect life, health, or property or who offer their services to the public. Registration generally requires a degree from an ABET-accredited engineering program, four years of relevant work experience, and passing a state examination. For more information on licensing and examination requirements, visit the National Council of Examiners for Engineering and Surveying's Web site, http://www.ncees.org.

Other Requirements

Certain characteristics help qualify a person for a career in mining engineering. These include the judgment to adapt knowledge to practical purposes, the imagination and analytical skill to solve problems, the ability to remain calm under pressure, and the capacity to predict the performance and cost of new processes or devices. Mining engineers must also be able to communicate effectively, work as part of a team, and supervise other workers.

EXPLORING

To learn about the profession of mining engineering, you may find it helpful to talk with science teachers and school counselors and with people employed in the minerals industry. You might also wish to read more about the industry and its engineers.

Companies and government agencies that employ graduates of mining engineering programs also hire undergraduates as part of a cooperative engineering education program. Students often enter such programs the summer preceding their junior year, after they have taken a certain number of engineering courses. They normally alternate terms of on-campus study and terms of work at the employer's facilities.

On the job, students assume the role of a junior mining engineer. They report to an experienced engineer, who acts as their supervisor and counselor. He or she assigns them work within their capabilities, evaluates their performance, and advises them as though they were permanent employees. Students have ample opportunity to interact with a diverse group of engineers and managers and to ask them about their work, their company, and mining engineering in general. Participation in the actual practice of the profession can help students assess their own aptitudes and interests and decide which courses will be most useful to them during the remainder of their engineering program.

EMPLOYERS

There are approximately 7,100 mining and geological engineers employed in the United States. Nearly 50 percent work in the mining industry itself; the others work for government agencies, engineering consulting firms, and in academia.

STARTING OUT

Beginning mining engineers generally perform routine tasks under the supervision of experienced engineers. Some mining companies provide starting engineers with in-house training. As engineers gain knowledge and experience, they receive increasingly difficult assignments along with greater independence to develop designs, solve problems, and make decisions.

ADVANCEMENT

Mining engineers may become directors of specific mining projects. Some head research projects. Mining engineers may go on to work as technical specialists or to supervise a team of engineers and technicians. Some eventually manage their mining company's engineering department or enter other managerial, management support, or sales positions.

EARNINGS

The U.S. Department of Labor (DOL) reports that median annual earnings of mining and geological engineers were $82,870 in 2010. Salaries ranged from less than $48,950 to $129,700 or more.

According to a 2009 salary survey by the National Association of Colleges and Employers, new graduates with bachelor's degrees in mining and mineral engineering received starting offers averaging $64,404 a year.

Engineers who work for the federal government in its mining operations tend to earn less than their counterparts in the private oil and gas industries.

Depending on their employers, most mining engineers enjoy a full complement of benefits, including vacation and sick time as well as holidays and medical and dental insurance.

WORK ENVIRONMENT

Engineers in the mining industry generally work where the mineral deposits are situated, often near small, rural communities. But those who specialize in research, management, consulting, or sales may work in metropolitan areas.

For those who work at the mine sites, conditions vary depending on the mine's location and structure and on what the engineer does. Conditions in the underground environment differ from those in surface mining. Natural light and fresh air are absent; temperatures may be uncomfortably hot or cold. Some mines have large amounts of water seeping into the openings. Potential hazards include caving ground, rockfalls, explosions from accumulation of gas or misuse of explosives, and poisonous gases. Most mines, however, are relatively safe and comfortable, owing to artificial light and ventilation, protective clothing, and water-pumping and ground-support systems.

Many mining engineers work a standard 40-hour week. In order to meet project deadlines, however, they may have to work longer hours under considerable stress.

OUTLOOK

The demand for mining engineers is expected to grow faster than the average for all careers through 2018, according to the DOL. Opportunities for mining engineers should be good for several reasons. Demand is increasing for coal, metals, minerals, as well as the demand for products made from stone, clay, and glass. Additionally, many mining engineers are nearing retirement age. Since few students major in mining engineering, and only a few schools offer mining engineering programs, these vacant positions may not be completely filled by new graduates. Finally, U.S. mining engineers are increasingly sought after to work on projects in foreign countries.

Mining engineers who are willing to work in foreign countries will have strong employment prospects.

Shortages in our natural resources will also create new opportunities for mining engineers. As mineral deposits are depleted, engineers will have to devise ways of mining less accessible low-grade ores to meet the demand for new alloys and new uses for minerals and metals. As more attention is placed on the environmental effects of mining, more engineers will be needed to provide expertise regarding land reclamation and water and air pollution.

FOR MORE INFORMATION

For information on careers, schools, college student membership, scholarships and grants, and other resources, contact
The Minerals, Metals, and Materials Society
184 Thorn Hill Road
Warrendale, PA 15086-7514
Tel: 800-759-4867
http://www.tms.org

For statistics on the mining industry, contact
National Mining Association
101 Constitution Avenue, NW, Suite 500 East
Washington, DC 20001-2133
Tel: 202-463-2600
http://www.nma.org

For information on educational programs, contact
Society for Mining, Metallurgy, and Exploration
12999 East Adam Aircraft Circle
Englewood, CO 80112-4167
Tel: 800-763-3132
http://www.smenet.org

For information on career opportunities, scholarships, and mentor programs, contact
Society of Women Engineers
120 South LaSalle Street, Suite 1515
Chicago, IL 60603-3572
Tel: 877-793-4636
E-mail: hq@swe.org
http://www.swe.org

Paleontologists

OVERVIEW

Paleontologists study the fossils of ancient life-forms, including human life, found in sedimentary rocks on or within the earth's crust. Paleontological analyses range from the description of large, easily visible features to biochemical analysis of incompletely fossilized tissue. The observations are used to infer relationships between past and present groups of organisms (taxonomy), to investigate the origins of life, and to investigate the ecology of the past (paleoecology) from which implications for the sustainability of life under present ecological conditions can be drawn. Paleontology is usually considered a subspecialty of the larger field of geology.

HISTORY

During Europe's Renaissance, the artist and scientist Leonardo da Vinci, among others, established that fossils were the natural remains of organic creatures, and in the middle of the 17th century, Nicolaus Steno of Denmark wrote a treatise proposing that sedimentary rocks were laid down in layers, with the oldest at the bottom. The physical description of fossils was permissible as long as it did not lead to dissonant conclusions regarding the age of the earth. As an example, the early 17th century saw the naming and characterization of the trilobites, an extinct but very large group of marine arthropods once abundant everywhere in the seas and, as a group, of far greater longevity than the dinosaurs. When fossil evidence was used to advance a history of the earth that contradicted a literal reading of the Bible, however, the penalties were severe.

A paleontologist studies fossilized bones of juvenile hadrosaurs—
duckbilled, plant-eating dinosaurs that grew to 10 feet tall and 40 feet
long. *(Al Grillo, AP Photo)*

The Age of Enlightenment in Europe sped up religion's waning grip on the interpretation of science, and paleontology as a scientific discipline may be considered to have started in the early 1800s. In the young republic of the United States, Thomas Jefferson, then vice president, in 1797 published one of the first papers on American fossil vertebrates; he also named a gigantic ground sloth that once roamed over much of the United States *Megalonyx jeffersonii*. At this time there was considerable congress between natural historians in Europe, Great Britain, and the United States, each eager to learn of the other's latest findings and theories. The 19th century was also the age of the quintessential "gentleman explorer," whose travels overlapped in time with government-sponsored exploring expeditions to all parts of the globe. The number of specimens returned

Profile: Paul Sereno (1957–)

Paul Sereno is really good at finding dinosaur bones. In fact, this well-known paleontologist has discovered the remains of dinosaurs on five continents. These range from *Suchomimu*, a fish-eating dinosaur; to *Afrovenator*, a 27-foot-long meat-eater, to *Carcharodontosaurus*, a gigantic meat-eating dinosaur. Sereno and his team also found the remains of *Sarcosuchus*, the largest crocodile that ever lived on earth.

Sereno traces his love of dinosaurs to a behind-the-scenes museum tour he took as a child. Since then, he has been hooked on paleontology, a field of study that combines geology, biology, and adventure. Sereno studied geology at Columbia University and the American Museum of Natural History in New York. In 1987, he joined the University of Chicago, teaching paleontology, evolution, and human anatomy. In 1997, Sereno received the Walker Prize for extraordinary contributions in paleontology from the Boston Museum of Science. In 1999, he received Columbia University's University Medal for Excellence.

Sereno is also a co-founder of Project Exploration, a nonprofit organization that brings a unique approach to the study of science to many of Chicago's inner-city minority students—especially girls. Project Exploration's after-school and summer programs offers immersion into the field of paleontology, girls' science conferences, and science and leadership opportunities. Visit www.project exploration.org for more information.

Sources: PaulSereno.org, ProjectExploration.org

from these expeditions led to the founding of many of the great natural history museums. In the middle of this activity, Charles Darwin boarded the *Beagle* for a multiyear voyage of exploration and natural observation, resulting in his writing *On the Origin of Species by Means of Natural Selection* in 1859, a major contribution to the blossoming of paleontology.

Contemporary paleontology is modeled on an understanding of life-forms as related in extended family trees, some of very ancient origin. In detailing ancestral and modern lineage, paleontologists want to know the precise physical, chemical, and nutritional environment that supported life and what changes in this environment forced some creatures into extinction while allowing others to thrive.

THE JOB

Paleontologists broadly classify themselves according to the life-form studied. *Palynologists* study tiny to submicroscopic life-forms, such as pollen or plankton. Microfossils may be of plant or animal origin and are extremely abundant. *Paleobotanists* study macroscopic fossil plants.

In the animal kingdom, *vertebrate paleontologists* study animals with a backbone, among them the classes of fishes, birds, reptiles, and mammals. Each area of specialization requires extensive knowledge of the anatomy, ecology, and habits of modern representatives of the class. *Invertebrate paleontologists* study animals without a backbone, such as the classes of insects, sponges, corals, and trilobites. Invertebrate paleontologists are especially useful to the oil industry, for fossil plankton taken from drilling cores are an indication of the age of the rocks and of the formations in which oil reservoirs are likely to be concentrated. The mining and minerals industry also hires *stratigraphers* and *petrographers*, who study the distribution and content of rock layers to identify subsurface mineral deposits. These scientists helped to discover rare quarries of limestone in Indiana and other areas. This limestone, composed of the skeletal remains of tiny fossilized creatures, has provided impressive amounts of building material. However, the mining and minerals industry has few positions for paleontologists.

When conducting paleontological research, scientists' analyses begin with careful measurement and anatomical description of fossils, accompanied, if possible, by drawings showing what the three-dimensional creatures may have looked like in life. The fossils then are dated and placed in a physical context. Dating may entail both laboratory analyses and comparisons with fossil beds of known age or a comparison with stratigraphic layers of rock in different forma-tions around the world. In the third step, the fossils and the forma-tions in which they occurred are used to construct a history of earth on either a small, local scale or a large scale. Large-scale events that can be reconstructed from fossil evidence include the uplift, tilting, and erosion of mountain ranges, the rise and subsidence of seas, and movements of landmasses over geological time. In the fourth step, fossils are used as evidence of life to fill in missing links in the fos-sil record, to revise taxonomic classifications, and to construct the biology of descent of living organisms.

Museum curators are linked to the fourth phase of paleonto-logical analysis, for virtually all contemporary *geology curators* are evolutionists. Museum curators typically hold a doctorate and have done considerable independent research; these positions are highly competitive. Geology curators must raise grant funding to support themselves and a work crew in the field, and some have teaching responsibilities in joint programs of study with universities as well. Collection managers in geology usually have a minimum of a mas-ter's degree; some have doctorates. *Geology collection managers* study, catalogue, and maintain the museum's collection, ship speci-mens to external researchers for study, and sometimes participate in fieldwork. Ordinarily there is one collection manager for the geol-ogy holdings, but occasionally there is more than one. In that case, the duties may be divided among vertebrate mammals, invertebrate mammals, fossil amphibians and reptiles, fossil birds, and fossil plants. Collection managers are generalists and work as colleagues with curators.

Some paleontologists work as *college teachers*. To teach at this level, they must have a doctorate or be a candidate for a doctor-ate. Their primary educational responsibilities are divided between teaching undergraduate courses in earth science and advanced semi-nars in paleontology. In addition to in-class duties, they must also prepare lessons and curriculum, prepare tests, meet with students during office hours, and attend department meetings. They also conduct personal research, focusing on any area of the field that interests them.

Although the preponderance of paleontological research is car-ried out on land, marine fossil beds are of great interest. The cost of mounting an expedition to extract samples of sedimentary rock from the deep-sea floor usually means that the sponsoring institu-tion must procure sizable support from industry or the government. Some paleontologists work in the oil industry to develop offshore wells; a few find employment with oceanographic institutes.

REQUIREMENTS

High School
Supplement your high school's college prep program with additional courses in the sciences and mathematics, including advanced classes in biology, chemistry, algebra, and trigonometry. Paleontologists rely a great deal on computer programs and databases, so take courses in computers and programming. You will be preparing your findings for publication and presentation, so take English and speech classes. Foreign language classes will also be valuable, as you may be conducting research in other countries.

Postsecondary Training
Paleontology is a subspecialty of geology or, less commonly, of botany, zoology, or physical anthropology. In college, you will major in geology or biology. The college curriculum for a geology major includes mathematics through calculus, chemistry, physics, and life sciences, with additional seminars in the specialty area and in the history of science.

Because paleontology is a specialty area encountered only briefly during the undergraduate curriculum, you should anticipate graduate training. In fact, most scientists in the field find that a doctorate is necessary simply to have time to gain the substantial knowledge base and independent research skills necessary in their field.

Other Requirements
You should be inquisitive, with a natural curiosity about the world and its history. A desire to read and study is also important, as you will be spending many years in school. It is important to have a respect for other cultures, as you may be working closely with professionals from other countries. Good organizational skills will help you in your work with fossils and museum collections. People skills are also very important, as you'll be relying on personal contacts in your pursuit of work and funding.

EXPLORING

An estimated 55,000 amateur rock hounds belong to organized clubs in the United States, and an untold additional number with no formal group membership also delight in fossil hunting in areas open to the public. You should locate and join one of these clubs and/or take fossil-hunting expeditions and visits to museums on your own. Local museums with a strong geology component frequently conduct field trips that are open to the public.

The Midwest and Great Plains states are especially rich in fossil beds, owing to the inland sea that once overlay these areas and whose sediments protected the skeletal remains of creatures from predation or being moved about. Professional geology societies publish brochures on fossil hunting and the kinds of fossils available in different locales. State geological societies, often housed on the main campus of state universities, are excellent sources of information. Earthwatch Institute is an organization that involves people with various environmental projects, including the mammoth graveyard fossil excavation site of Hot Springs, South Dakota, and the Late Triassic period excavation site at the Ischigualasto-Talampaya World Heritage Site in Argentina.

EMPLOYERS

Most paleontologists work in colleges and universities as faculty of paleontology and geology programs. They also find work in museums and with government research projects. The petroleum industry was once a great source of jobs for paleontologists, but these jobs, though still available, are fewer in number. Some paleontologists are self-employed, offering their expertise as consultants.

STARTING OUT

As an undergraduate, you may be able to work as an intern or volunteer in the geology department of a local museum. You may also be able to participate in fieldwork as a paying member of an expedition. Such an arrangement is usually worked out personally with the expedition leader. These entry-level positions may lead to admission to graduate programs and even to employment after advanced degrees are earned. The American Geological Institute and the Geological Society of America offer some internship and scholarship opportunities.

You will rely mostly on personal contacts when seeking a job after receiving a graduate degree. Networking with others in paleontology, especially your college professors, can allow you to meet those who can direct you to job openings and research opportunities.

ADVANCEMENT

Advancement depends on where the paleontologist is employed. Universities and museums follow a typical assistant, associate, and senior (or full) professorial or curatorial track, with the requirements for advancement very similar: research and publishing, education, and service to the institution. Advancement in museum work may also depend on the acquisition of a doctorate. Advancement in state and federal surveys requires research and publishing. In federal employment and in industry, mechanisms for advancement are likely to be spelled out by the employer. Government-sponsored research and term positions are the least stable avenues of work, because of their temporary nature and dependence on a source of funding that may not be renewed.

Many paleontologists remain active in the field beyond the date of formal retirement, procuring independent research funds to support their activities or developing an unpaid association with a neighboring university to gain access to collections and laboratory facilities. The low-tech nature of geological fieldwork allows basic field studies to be conducted fairly inexpensively. Others become consultants to geoscientific firms.

EARNINGS

According to the U.S. Department of Labor, all geoscientists, including paleontologists, earned a median annual salary of $82,500 in 2010. The lowest paid 10 percent earned $43,800 and the highest paid 10 percent earned $160,910 or more annually. College earth science teachers (including those who specialize in paleontology) had median annual salaries of $78,660 in 2009. Salaries ranged from less than $43,350 to more than $133,080. A 2009 salary survey from the American Association of Petroleum Geologists found that geoscientists working in the petroleum industry with three to five years of experience and a bachelor's degree had average annual earnings of $99,800. Salaries increase with a person's years of experience and level of education. Those with 10 to 14 years experience and holding master's degrees averaged $127,400. Those with Ph.D.'s and many years of experience had annual earnings of $169,600 or more.

Once these highly trained scientists have entered the field, they usually receive excellent benefits packages and ample vacation time and sick leave. In addition, paleontologists who travel to various locations for their research have their travel and accommodations paid for and receive travel stipends from their employer or funding source.

WORK ENVIRONMENT

The day-to-day activities of a paleontologist vary, but, in the course of a year usually involve some mix of fieldwork, laboratory analysis, library research, and grant writing or teaching. In industry, a paleontologist's duties may be defined by the project the company has developed. In academia and in museum work, a paleontologist may be able to define a personal course of research but may have less time for that research because of teaching or administrative responsibilities.

Paleontological study is international in scope and impressive in the sweep of time it commands. Because the fossil-bearing strata of interest to paleontologists occur in widely separated localities, U.S. paleontologists may undertake extensive correspondence or joint fieldwork with colleagues throughout the world. In addition, paleontology is a living science, with new plant and animal species extracted from the rocks every year and corresponding new biological relationships waiting to be explored. The depth and breadth of paleontological study and its ever clearer relationship to contemporary ecological concerns make it an attractive profession for those interested in a larger view of life.

OUTLOOK

More paleontologists graduate each year than there are available positions, and consequently many paleontologists are unemployed or underemployed. Federal and state surveys absorb a small number of new graduates with baccalaureate or master's degrees but cannot accommodate all those seeking work.

To increase the likelihood of employment, students will find it helpful to pursue high academic standards, including, if possible, independent research and publication during the advanced degree years, cross-training in a related field, such as zoology or botany, and planning a broad-based career that combines knowledge of government activities, industry experience, and teaching and research.

FOR MORE INFORMATION

For information on careers in the geological sciences, as well as information about scholarships and internships, contact
American Geological Institute
4220 King Street
Alexandria, VA 22302-1502
Tel: 703-379-2480
http://www.agiweb.org

For recommended readings, information on internships, and geoscience news, visit the GSA Web site.
Geological Society of America (GSA)
PO Box 9140
Boulder, CO 80301-9140
Tel: 888-443-4472
E-mail: gsaservice@geosociety.org
http://www.geosociety.org

For general information on paleontology and internships, contact
Paleontological Research Institution
1259 Trumansburg Road
Ithaca, NY 14850-1313
Tel: 607-273-6623
http://www.museumoftheearth.org

For information on careers and graduate training, contact
The Society of Vertebrate Paleontology
111 Deer Lake Road, Suite 100
Deerfield, IL 60015-4943
Tel: 847-480-9095
http://www.vertpaleo.org

INTERVIEW

Dr. Jørn Hurum is a paleontologist and associate professor in vertebrate paleontology at the University of Oslo, in Oslo, Norway. He discussed his career with the editors of Careers in Focus: Geology.

Q. What made you want to become a paleontologist?

A. When I was about six years old my parents read a book to me. The book was about a boy walking along a gravel road throwing rocks. He picked up a rock and the rock spoke to him. The fossil in the rock said "Do not throw me away. I am a trilobite, and I have a story to tell." And then a long story about fossils as the clues to the evolution of life started. As a child, I was philosophical. I asked myself questions such as "Why am I me and not somebody else?" and "Where do we come from?" I understood that fossils were clues to these questions, and I wanted to learn everything about them. This journey will be the task of my life.

Q. What is one thing that young people may not know about a career in paleontology?

A. Paleontology is fun, but it does not pay very well. There are fewer than a hundred dinosaur researchers (and positions) in the world; most paleontologists study other types of fossils. They study microfossils and are doing research to find oil or studying past climates.

Q. What are the most important personal and professional qualities for paleontologists?

A. You need to be able to push yourself; working as a paleontologist can be quite a lonely job sometimes. And you need the ability to be completely absorbed in your work and not be distracted by minor political problems at work.

Q. What are some of the pros and cons of your job?

A. It is hard to get a permanent position, but if you are lucky, working as a paleontologist is the best job in the world if you like fossils.

Q. What advice would you give to young people who are interested in the field?

A. If you are completely dedicated to studying fossils, but told by people not to pursue education in the field because it is hard to get a job, do not listen to them. Follow your dreams and do it. The best workers will always get interesting jobs.

Petroleum Engineers

OVERVIEW

Petroleum engineers apply the principles of geology, physics, and the engineering sciences to the recovery, development, and processing of petroleum. As soon as an exploration team has located an area that could contain oil or gas, petroleum engineers begin their work, which includes determining the best location for drilling new wells, as well as the economic feasibility of developing them. They are also involved in operating oil and gas facilities, monitoring and forecasting reservoir performance, and utilizing enhanced oil recovery techniques that extend the life of wells. There are approximately 21,900 petroleum engineers employed in the United States.

HISTORY

Within a broad perspective, the history of petroleum engineering can be traced back hundreds of millions of years to when the remains of plants and animals blended with sand and mud and transformed into rock. It is from this ancient underground rock that petroleum is taken, for the organic matter of the plants and animals decomposed into oil during these millions of years and accumulated into pools deep underground.

In primitive times, people did not know how to drill for oil; instead, they collected the liquid substance after it had seeped to above-ground surfaces. Petroleum is known to have been used at that time for caulking ships and for concocting medicines.

Petroleum engineering as we know it today was not established until the mid-1800s, an incredibly long time after the fundamental

QUICK FACTS

School Subjects
Mathematics
Physics

Personal Skills
Helping/teaching
Technical/scientific

Work Environment
Indoors and outdoors
One location with some travel

Minimum Education Level
Bachelor's degree

Salary Range
$63,480 to $114,080 to $186,800+

Certification or Licensing
Voluntary (certification)
Required for certain positions (licensing)

Outlook
Faster than the average

DOT
010

GOE
02.07.04

NOC
2145

O*NET-SOC
17-2171.00

ingredients of petroleum were deposited within the earth. In 1859, the American Edwin Drake was the first person to ever pump the so-called rock oil from under the ground, an endeavor that, before its success, was laughed at and considered impossible. Forward-thinking investors, however, had believed in the operation and thought that underground oil could be used as inexpensive fluid for lighting lamps and for lubricating machines (and therefore could make them rich). The drilling of the first well, in Titusville, Pennsylvania (1869), ushered in a new worldwide era: the oil age.

At the turn of the century, petroleum was being distilled into kerosene, lubricants, and wax. Gasoline was considered a useless by-product and was run off into rivers as waste. However, this changed with the invention of the internal combustion engine and the automobile. By 1915 there were more than half a million cars in the United States, virtually all of them powered by gasoline.

Edwin Drake's drilling operation struck oil 70 feet below the ground. Since that time, technological advances have been made, and the professional field of petroleum engineering has been established. Today's operations drill as far down as six miles. Because the United States began to rely so much on oil, the country contributed significantly to creating schools and educational programs in this engineering discipline. The world's first petroleum engineering curriculum was devised in the United States in 1914. Today, there are fewer than 30 U.S. and Canadian universities that offer petroleum engineering degrees. The first schools were concerned mainly with developing effective methods of locating oil sites and with devising efficient machinery for drilling wells. Over the years, as sites have been depleted, engineers have been more concerned with formulating methods for extracting as much oil as possible from each well. Today's petroleum engineers focus on issues such as computerized drilling operations; however, because usually only about 40 to 60 percent of each site's oil is extracted, engineers must still deal with designing optimal conditions for maximum oil recovery.

THE JOB

Petroleum engineer is a rather generalized title that encompasses several specialties, each one playing an important role in ensuring the safe and productive recovery of oil and natural gas. In general, petroleum engineers are involved in the entire process of oil recovery, from preliminary steps, such as analyzing cost factors, to the last stages, such as monitoring the production rate and then repacking the well after it has been depleted.

Petroleum engineering is closely related to the separate engineering discipline of geoscience engineering. Before petroleum engineers can begin work on an oil reservoir, prospective sites must be sought by *geological engineers*, along with *geologists* and *geophysicists*. These scientists determine whether a site has potential oil. Petroleum engineers develop plans for drilling. Drilling is usually unsuccessful, with eight out of 10 test wells being "dusters" (dry wells) and only one of the remaining two test wells having enough oil to be commercially producible. When a significant amount of oil is discovered, engineers can begin their work of maximizing oil production at the site. The development company's *engineering manager* oversees the activities of the various petroleum engineering specialties, including reservoir engineers, drilling engineers, and production engineers.

Reservoir engineers use the data gathered by the previous geoscience studies and estimate the actual amount of oil that will be extracted from the reservoir. It is the reservoir engineers who determine whether the oil will be taken by primary methods (simply pumping the oil from the field) or by enhanced methods (using additional energy such as water pressure to force the oil up). The reservoir engineer is responsible for calculating the cost of the recovery process relative to the expected value of the oil produced and simulates future performance using sophisticated computer models. Besides performing studies of existing company-owned oil fields, reservoir engineers also evaluate fields the company is thinking of buying.

Drilling engineers work with geologists and drilling contractors to design and supervise drilling operations. They are the engineers involved with the actual drilling of the well. They ask: What will be the best methods for penetrating the earth? It is the responsibility of these workers to supervise the building of the derrick (a platform, constructed over the well, that holds the hoisting devices), choose the equipment, and plan the drilling methods. Drilling engineers must have a thorough understanding of the geological sciences so that they can know, for instance, how much stress to place on the rock being drilled.

Production engineers determine the most efficient methods and equipment to optimize oil and gas production. For example, they establish the proper pumping unit configuration and perform tests to determine well fluid levels and pumping load. They plan field workovers and well stimulation techniques such as secondary and tertiary recovery (for example, injecting steam, water, or a special recovery fluid) to maximize field production.

Various research personnel are involved in this field; some are more specialized than others. They include the *research chief engineer*, who directs studies related to the design of new drilling and production methods, the *oil-well equipment research engineer*, who directs research to design improvements in oil-well machinery and devices, and the *oil-field equipment test engineer*, who conducts experiments to determine the effectiveness and safety of these improvements.

In addition to all of the above, sales personnel play an important part in the petroleum industry. *Oil-well equipment and services sales engineers* sell various types of equipment and devices used in all stages of oil recovery. They provide technical support and service to their clients, including oil companies and drilling contractors.

REQUIREMENTS

High School

In high school, you can prepare for college engineering programs by taking courses in mathematics, physics, chemistry, geology, and computer science. Economics, history, and English are also highly recommended because these subjects will improve your communication and management skills. Mechanical drawing and foreign languages are also helpful.

Postsecondary Training

A bachelor's degree in engineering is the minimum requirement. In college, you can follow either a specific petroleum engineering curriculum or a program in a closely related field, such as geophysics or mining engineering. In the United States and Canada, there are fewer than 30 universities and colleges that offer programs that concentrate on petroleum engineering, many of which are located in California and Texas. The first two years toward the bachelor of science degree involve the study of many of the same subjects taken in high school, only at an advanced level, as well as basic engineering courses. In the junior and senior years, students take more specialized courses: geology, formation evaluation, properties of reservoir rocks and fluids, well drilling, properties of reservoir fluids, petroleum production, and reservoir analysis.

Because the technology changes so rapidly, many petroleum engineers continue their education to receive a master's degree and then a doctorate. Petroleum engineers who have earned advanced degrees command higher salaries and often are eligible for better advancement opportunities. Those who work in research and teaching positions are usually required to have these higher credentials.

Students considering an engineering career in the petroleum industry should be aware that the industry employs all kinds of engineers. People with chemical, electrical, geoscience, mechanical, environmental, and other engineering degrees are also employed in this field.

The Society of Petroleum Engineers offers a list of postsecondary petroleum engineering programs at its Web site, http://www.spe.org.

Certification or Licensing

The Society of Petroleum Engineers offers voluntary certification to petroleum engineers who meet education and experience requirements and pass an examination. Contact the society for more information.

Many jobs, especially public projects, require that the engineer be licensed as a professional engineer. To be licensed, candidates must have a degree from an engineering program accredited by the Accreditation Board for Engineering and Technology. Additional requirements for obtaining the license vary from state to state, but all applicants must take an exam and have several years of related experience on the job or in teaching. For more information on licensing and examination requirements, visit http://www.ncees.org.

Other Requirements

Students thinking about this career should enjoy science and math. You need to be a creative problem solver who likes to come up with new ways to get things done and try them out. You need to be curious, wanting to know why and how things are done. You also need to be a logical thinker with a capacity for detail, and you must be a good communicator who can work well with others.

EXPLORING

One of the most satisfying ways to explore this occupation is to participate in Junior Engineering Technical Society (JETS) programs. JETS participants enter engineering design and problem-solving contests and learn team development skills, often with an engineering mentor. Science fairs and clubs also offer fun and challenging ways to learn about engineering.

Certain students are able to attend summer programs held at colleges and universities that focus on material not traditionally offered in high school. Usually these programs include recreational activities such as basketball, swimming, and track and field. For example, Worcester Polytechnic Institute offers the Frontiers program, a two-week residential session for high school seniors. For more information, visit http://www.wpi.edu/admissions/undergraduate/visit/frontiers.html. The American Indian Science and Engineering

Society (AISES) also sponsors mathematics and science camps that are open to Native American students and held at various college campuses. For more information, visit http://www.aises.org.

Talking with someone who has worked as a petroleum engineer would also be a very helpful and inexpensive way to explore this field. One good way to find an experienced person to talk to is through Internet sites that feature career areas to explore, industry message boards, and mailing lists.

You can also explore this career by touring oilfields or corporate sites (contact the public relations department of oil companies for more information), or you can try to land a temporary or summer job in the petroleum industry on a drilling and production crew. Trade journals, high school counselors, the career services office at technical or community colleges, and the associations listed at the end of this article are other helpful resources that will help you learn more about the career of petroleum engineer.

EMPLOYERS

Petroleum engineers are employed by major oil companies, as well as smaller oil companies. They work in oil exploration and production. Some petroleum engineers are employed by consulting companies and equipment suppliers. The federal government is also an employer of engineers. In the United States, oil or natural gas is produced in 42 states, with most sites located in California, Louisiana, Oklahoma, and Texas, plus offshore regions. Many other engineers work in other oil-producing areas such as the Arctic Circle, China's Tarim Basin, and the Middle East. Approximately 21,900 petroleum engineers are employed in the United States.

STARTING OUT

The most common and perhaps the most successful way to obtain a petroleum engineering job is to apply for positions through the career services office at the college you attend. Oil companies often have recruiters who seek potential graduates while they are in their last year of engineering school.

Applicants are also advised to simply check the job sections of major newspapers and apply directly to companies seeking employees. They should also keep informed of the general national employment outlook in this industry by reading trade and association journals, such as the Society of Petroleum Engineers' *Journal of Petroleum Technology* (http://www.spe.org/spe-app/spe/jpt/index.htm).

Engineering internships and co-op programs where students attend classes for a portion of the year and then work in an engineering-related job for the remainder of the year allow students to graduate with valuable work experience sought by employers. Many times these students are employed full time after graduation at the place where they had their internship or co-op job.

As in most engineering professions, entry-level petroleum engineers first work under the supervision of experienced professionals for a number of years. New engineers usually are assigned to a field location where they learn different aspects of field petroleum engineering. Initial responsibilities may include well productivity, reservoir and enhanced recovery studies, production equipment and application design, efficiency analyses, and economic evaluations. Field assignments are followed by other opportunities in regional and headquarters offices.

ADVANCEMENT

After several years working under professional supervision, engineers can begin to move up to higher levels. Workers often formulate a plan for their advancement during their first years on the job. In the operations division, petroleum engineers can work their way up from the field to district, division, and then operations manager. Some engineers work through various engineering positions from field engineer to staff, then division, and finally chief engineer on a project. Some engineers may advance into top executive management. In any position, however, continued enrollment in educational courses is usually required to keep abreast of technological progress and changes. After about four years of work experience, engineers usually apply for a Professional Engineer license so they can be certified to work on a larger number of projects.

Others earn their master's or doctoral degree so they can advance to more prestigious research engineering, university-level teaching, or consulting positions. Also, petroleum engineers may transfer to many other occupations, such as economics, environmental management, and groundwater hydrology. Finally, some entrepreneurial-minded workers become independent operators and owners of their own oil companies.

EARNINGS

Petroleum engineers with a bachelor's degree earned average starting salaries of $83,121 in July 2009, according to the National Association of Colleges and Employers. A survey by the Society of Petroleum Engineers reports the following average salaries in 2009 for members by years of experience: zero to 10 years, $87,600; six to nine years, $121,700; 15 to 19 years, $150,000; and 25 or more years, $186,800.

The U.S. Department of Labor (DOL) reports that petroleum engineers earned median annual salaries of $114,080 in 2010. Salaries ranged from less than $63,480 to $166,400 or more.

Salary rates tend to reflect the economic health of the petroleum industry as a whole. When the price of oil is high, salaries can be expected to grow; low oil prices often result in stagnant wages.

Fringe benefits for petroleum engineers are good. Most employers provide health and accident insurance, sick pay, retirement plans, profit-sharing plans, and paid vacations. Education benefits are also competitive.

WORK ENVIRONMENT

Petroleum engineers work all over the world: the high seas, remote jungles, vast deserts, plains, and mountain ranges. Petroleum engineers who are assigned to remote foreign locations may be separated from their families for long periods of time or be required to resettle their families when new job assignments arise. Those working overseas may live in company-supplied housing.

Some petroleum engineers, such as drilling engineers, work primarily out in the field at or near drilling sites in all kinds of weather and environments. The work can be dirty and dangerous. Responsibilities such as making reports, conducting studies of data, and analyzing costs are usually tended to in offices either away from the site or in temporary work trailers.

Other engineers work in offices in cities of varying sizes, with only occasional visits to an oil field. Research engineers work in laboratories much of the time, while those who work as professors spend most of their time on campuses. Workers involved in economics, management, consulting, and government service tend to spend their work time exclusively indoors.

OUTLOOK

Employment for petroleum engineers is expected to grow faster than the average for all careers through 2018, according to the DOL. There will be good opportunities for petroleum engineers because the number of degrees granted in petroleum engineering is low, leaving more job openings than there are qualified candidates.

Employment opportunities will become even better if the federal government constructs new gas refineries, pipelines, and transmission lines, as well as drills in areas that were previously off-limits to such development.

Cost-effective technology that permits new drilling and increases production from existing resources will continue to be essential in the profitability of the oil industry. Therefore, petroleum engineers will continue to have a vital role to play, even in this age of streamlined operations and company restructurings.

FOR MORE INFORMATION

Visit the association's Web site for information on careers and membership for college students, as well as answers to frequently asked questions about the field.

American Association of Petroleum Geologists
1444 South Boulder
Tulsa, OK 74119-3604
Tel: 800-364-2274
http://www.aapg.org

The institute represents the professional interests of oil and natural gas companies. Visit its Web site for career information and facts and statistics about the petroleum industry.

American Petroleum Institute
1220 L Street, NW
Washington, DC 20005-4070
Tel: 202-682-8000
http://www.api.org

For information about JETS programs, products, and engineering career brochures (in a variety of disciplines), contact

Junior Engineering Technical Society (JETS)
1420 King Street, Suite 405
Alexandria, VA 22314-2750
Tel: 703-548-5387
E-mail: info@jets.org
http://www.jets.org

For a list of petroleum technology schools and information on certification and careers in petroleum engineering, contact
Society of Petroleum Engineers
222 Palisades Creek Drive
Richardson, TX 75080-2040
Tel: 800-456-6863
E-mail: spedal@spe.org
http://www.spe.org

For information on career opportunities, scholarships, and mentor programs, contact
Society of Women Engineers
120 South LaSalle Street, Suite 1515
Chicago, IL 60603-3572
Tel: 877-793-4636
E-mail: hq@swe.org
http://www.swe.org

Petroleum Technicians

OVERVIEW

Petroleum technicians work in a wide variety of specialties in the petroleum industry. Many kinds of *drilling technicians* drill for petroleum from the earth and beneath the ocean. *Loggers* analyze rock cuttings from drilling and measure characteristics of rock layers. Various types of *production technicians* "complete" wells (prepare wells for production), collect petroleum from producing wells, and control production. *Engineering technicians* help improve drilling technology, maximize field production, and provide technical assistance. *Maintenance technicians* keep machinery and equipment running smoothly. There are approximately 15,200 petroleum and geological technicians employed in the United States.

HISTORY

In the 1950s and 1960s, the oil industry was relatively stable. Oil was cheap and much in demand. The international oil market was dominated by the "seven sisters"—Shell, Esso, BP, Gulf, Chevron, Texaco, and Mobil. However, by the end of the 1960s, Middle Eastern countries became more dominant. Many nationalized the major oil companies' operations or negotiated to control oil production. To promote and protect their oil production and revenues gained, Iran, Iraq, Kuwait, Saudi Arabia, and Venezuela (a country located in South America) formed OPEC (the Organization of Petroleum Exporting Countries). The Arab producers' policies during the Arab/Israeli War of 1973–74 and the Iranian Revolution in 1978 disrupted oil

QUICK FACTS

School Subjects
Mathematics
Physics

Personal Skills
Helping/teaching
Technical/scientific

Work Environment
Indoors and outdoors
Primarily multiple locations

Minimum Education Level
High school diploma

Salary Range
$29,950 to $54,020 to $99,860+

Certification or Licensing
None available

Outlook
Little or no change

DOT
010

GOE
02.05.01

NOC
2212

O*NET-SOC
19-4041.00, 19-4041.01, 19-4041.02, 47-5011.00, 47-5012.00, 47-5013.00, 47-5021.00

supplies and skyrocketed oil prices, indicating just how powerful OPEC had become.

By the early 1980s, economic recession and energy conservation measures had resulted in lower oil prices. There was—and still is—worldwide surplus production capacity. OPEC, which expanded membership to countries in the Far East and Africa, tried to impose quotas limiting production, with little success. In 1986, prices—which had once again risen—plummeted.

In the 1990s and 2000s, factors such as strong demand from a growing U.S. population, reductions in domestic oil exploration and production, and conflicts in oil-producing countries such as Iraq caused a significant increase in the price of petroleum.

The events of the 1960s through today have significantly altered the nation's attitude toward the price and availability of petroleum products. The federal government and domestic oil companies have come to realize that foreign sources of oil could easily be lost through regional conflicts or international tensions. To address this crisis, the U.S. government has set a goal of increased domestic production.

These developments have fostered great changes in the technology of oil drilling, in the science related to oil exploration, and in the management of existing oil fields. In many old abandoned fields, scientists found that nearly as much oil remained as had originally been produced from them by older methods. New technology is constantly being developed and used to find ways of extracting more of this remaining oil economically from old and new fields alike.

The career of petroleum technician was created to help the industry meet such challenges. Technological changes require scientifically

Facts About the Oil and Natural Gas Industries

- The U.S. oil and natural gas industries support 9.2 million American jobs.
- The U.S. oil industry produces nearly two billion barrels of oil annually.
- There are 165,000 miles of pipelines that move crude oil to refineries in the United States.
- There are 141 oil refineries in the United States.

Source: American Petroleum Institute

competent technical workers as crewmembers for well drilling and oil field management. Well-trained technicians are essential to the oil industry and will continue to be in the future.

THE JOB

Before petroleum technicians can begin work on an oil reservoir, prospective sites must first be sought by geological exploration teams. These crews perform seismic surveying, in which sound waves are created and their reflection from underground rocks recorded by seismographs, to help locate potential sources of oil. Other team members collect and examine geological data or test geological samples to determine petroleum and mineral content. They may also use surveying and mapping instruments and techniques to help locate and map test holes or the results of seismic tests.

It is the drill bit, however, that ultimately proves whether or not there is oil. Drilling for oil is a highly skilled operation involving many kinds of technicians: *rotary drillers, derrick operators, engine operators,* and *tool pushers.*

In the most common type of drilling, a drill bit with metal or diamond teeth is suspended on a drilling string consisting of 30-foot pipes joined together. The string is added as the bit goes deeper. The bit is turned either by a rotary mechanism on the drill floor or, increasingly, by a downhole motor. As drilling progresses, the bit gets worn and has to be replaced. The entire drilling string, sometimes weighing more than 100 tons, must be hauled to the surface and dismantled section by section, the bit replaced, then the string reassembled and run back down the well. Known as a "round trip," this operation can take the drilling crew most of a 12-hour shift in a deep well. Until recently, drill strings were mostly manually handled; however, mechanized drill rigs that handle pipe automatically have been introduced to improve safety and efficiency.

The driller directs the crew and is responsible for the machinery operation. The driller watches gauges and works throttles and levers to control the hoisting and rotation speed of the drill pipe and the amount of weight on the bit. Special care is needed as the bit nears oil and gas to avoid a "blow-out." Such "gushers" were common in the early days of the oil industry, but today's drilling technicians are trained to prevent them. Drillers also are responsible for recording the type and depth of strata penetrated each day and materials used.

Derrick operators are next in charge of the drilling crew. They work on a platform high up on the derrick and help handle the upper end of the drilling string during placement and removal. They also mix the special drilling "mud" that is pumped down through the pipe to lubricate and cool the bit as well as help control the flow of oil and gas when oil is struck.

Engine operators run engines to supply power for rotary drilling machinery and oversee their maintenance. They may help when the roughnecks pull or add pipe sections.

Tool pushers are in charge of one or more drilling rigs. They oversee erection of the rig, the selection of drill bits, the operation of drilling machinery, and the mixing of drilling mud. They arrange for the delivery of tools, machinery, fuel, water, and other supplies to the drilling site.

One very specialized drilling position is the *oil-well fishing-tool technician*. These technicians analyze conditions at wells where some object, or "fish," has obstructed the borehole. They direct the work of removing the obstacle (lost equipment or broken drill pipes, for example), choosing from a variety of techniques.

During drilling, *mud test technicians*, also called *mud loggers*, use a microscope at a portable laboratory on-site to analyze drill cuttings carried out of the well by the circulating mud for traces of oil. After final depth is reached, technicians called *well loggers* lower measuring devices to the bottom of the well on cable called wire-line. Wireline logs examine the electrical, acoustic, and radioactive properties of the rocks and provide information about rock type and porosity, and how much fluid (oil, gas, or water) it contains. These techniques, known as formation evaluation, help the operating company decide whether enough oil exists to warrant continued drilling.

The first well drilled is an exploration well. If oil is discovered, more wells, called appraisal wells, are drilled to establish the limits of the field. Then the field's economic worth and profit are evaluated. If it is judged economically worthwhile to develop the field, some of the appraisal wells may be used as production wells. The production phase of the operation deals with bringing the well fluids to the surface and preparing them for their trip through the pipeline to the refinery.

The first step is to complete the well—that is, to perform whatever operations are needed to start the well fluids flowing to the surface—and is performed by *well-servicing technicians*. These technicians use a variety of well-completion methods, determined by the oil reservoir's characteristics. Typical tasks include setting and cementing pipe (called production casing) so that the oil can come to the surface without leaking into the upper layers of rock. Well-servicing technicians may later perform maintenance work to improve or maintain the production from a formation already producing oil. These technicians bring in smaller rigs similar to drilling rigs for their work.

After the well has been completed, a structure consisting of control valves, pressure gauges, and chokes (called a Christmas tree because of the way its fittings branch out) is assembled at the top of the well to control the flow of oil and gas. Generally, production crews direct operations for several wells.

Well fluids are often a mixture of oil, gas, and water and must be separated and treated before going into the storage tanks. After separation, *treaters* apply heat, chemicals, electricity, or all three to remove contaminants. They also control well flow when the natural pressure is great enough to force oil from the well without pumping.

Pumpers operate, monitor, and maintain production facilities. They visually inspect well equipment to make sure it's functioning properly. They also detect and perform any routine maintenance needs. They adjust pumping cycle time to optimize production and measure the fluid levels in storage tanks, recording the information each day for entry on weekly gauge reports. Pumpers also advise oil haulers or purchasers when a tank is ready for sale.

Gaugers ensure that other company personnel and purchasers comply with the company's oil measurement and sale policy. They spotcheck oil measurements and resolve any discrepancies. They also check pumpers' equipment for accuracy and arrange for the replacement of malfunctioning gauging equipment.

Once a field has been brought into production, good reservoir management is needed to ensure that as much oil as possible is recovered. *Production engineering technicians* work with the production engineers to plan field workovers and well stimulation techniques such as secondary and tertiary recovery (for example, injecting steam, water, or a special recovery fluid) to maximize field production. *Reservoir engineering technicians* provide technical assistance to reservoir engineers. They prepare spreadsheets for analyses required for economic evaluations and forecasts. They also gather production data and maintain well histories and decline curves on both company-operated and outside-operated wells.

The petroleum industry has a need for other kinds of technicians as well, including *geological technicians*, *chemical technicians*, and *civil engineering technicians*.

REQUIREMENTS

All petroleum technician jobs require at least a high school diploma, and a few specialties require at least a bachelor's degree.

High School

If you are interested in this field, you should begin preparing in high school by taking algebra, geometry, trigonometry, and calculus classes. Earth science, chemistry, and physics are other useful subjects. High school courses in drafting, mechanics, or auto shop are also valuable preparation, especially for drilling and production technicians. Computer skills are particularly important for engineering technicians, as are typing and English courses.

Postsecondary Training

As mentioned above, postsecondary training is required for only a few petroleum technician positions. For example, a mud test technician must have at least a bachelor's degree in geology. Although postsecondary training is not usually required for drilling, production, or engineering technicians, these workers can gain familiarity with specified basic processes through special education in technical or community colleges. Postsecondary training can also help entry-level workers compete with experienced workers.

Petroleum technology programs, located primarily at schools in the West and Southwest, are helpful both for newcomers to the field and for those trying to upgrade their job skills. An associate's degree in applied science can be earned by completing a series of technical and education courses.

Petroleum technology programs provide training in drilling operations, fluids, and equipment; production methods; formation evaluation along with the basics of core analysis; and well completion methods and petroleum property evaluation, including evaluation of production history data and basic theories and techniques of economic analysis. These programs emphasize practical applications in the laboratory, field trips, and summer employment, as available.

Specialized training programs designed for oil company employees are offered by the suppliers of the special materials, equipment, or services.

Other Requirements

Petroleum technicians must be able to work with accuracy and precision; mistakes can be costly or hazardous to the technician and to others in the workplace. You should also be able to work both independently and as part of a team, display manual dexterity and mathematical aptitude, and be willing to work irregular hours.

Much of the work in the petroleum industry involves physical labor and is potentially dangerous. Field technicians must be strong and healthy, enjoy the outdoors in all weather, and be flexible and adaptable about working conditions and hours. Drilling crews may be away from their home base for several days at a time, while technicians on offshore rigs must be able to deal with a restricted environment for several days at a time. Petroleum technicians must also like working with machinery, scientific equipment and instruments, and computers. In addition, petroleum technicians must have good eyesight and hearing and excellent hand, eye, and body coordination.

Some technicians must operate off-road vehicles to transport people, supplies, and equipment to drilling and production sites. Most of this task is learned on the job after formal training is completed.

Some petroleum technicians require additional safety training, including hazardous materials training and first-aid training. In some cases, special physical examinations and drug testing are required. Testing and examinations generally take place after technicians are hired.

EXPLORING

You may want to investigate petroleum technician occupations further by checking your school or public libraries for books on the petroleum industry. Other resources include trade journals, high school counselors, the career services office at technical or community colleges, and the associations and Web sites listed at the end of this article. If you live near an oil field, you may be able to arrange a tour by contacting the public relations department of oil companies or drilling contractors.

Summer and other temporary jobs on drilling and production crews are excellent ways of finding out about this field. Temporary work can provide you with firsthand knowledge of the basics of oil field operations, equipment maintenance, safety, and other aspects of the work. You may also want to consider entering a two-year training program in petroleum technology to learn about the field.

EMPLOYERS

Although drilling for oil and gas is conducted in 42 states, nearly 75 percent of workers in this field are employed in four states: California, Louisiana, Oklahoma, and Texas. Employers in the crude petroleum and natural gas industry include major oil companies and independent producers. The oil and gas field services industry, which includes drilling contractors, logging companies, and well servicing contractors, is the other major source of employment.

Approximately 15,200 petroleum and geological technicians are employed in the United States.

STARTING OUT

You may enter the field of petroleum drilling or production as a laborer or general helper if you have completed high school. From there, you can work your way up to highly skilled technical jobs, responsibilities, and rewards.

Engineering technicians might start out as *engineering* or *production secretaries* and advance to the position of technician after two to five years of on-the-job experience and demonstrated competency in the use of computers.

Other technicians, such as mud test loggers or well loggers, will need a geology degree first. Upon obtaining your degree, you may start out as an assistant to experienced geologists or petroleum engineers.

Generally speaking, industry recruiters from major companies and employers regularly visit the career services offices of schools with petroleum technology programs and hire technicians before they finish their last year of technical school or college.

Because many graduates have little or no experience with well drilling operations, new technicians work primarily as assistants to the leaders of the operations. They may also help with the semi-skilled or skilled work in order to become familiar with the skills and techniques needed.

It is not uncommon, however, for employers to hire newly graduated technicians and immediately send them to a specialized training program. These programs are designed for oil company employees and usually are offered by the suppliers of the special materials, equipment, or services. After the training period, technicians may be sent anywhere in the world where the company has exploratory drilling or production operations.

ADVANCEMENT

In oil drilling and production, field advancement comes with experience and on-the-job competency. Although a petroleum technology degree is generally not required, it is clearly helpful in today's competitive climate. On a drilling crew, the usual job progression is as follows: from roughneck or rig builder to derrick operator, rotary driller, to tool pusher, and finally, oil production manager. In production, pumpers and gaugers may later become oil company production foremen or operations foremen; from there, they may proceed to operations management, which oversees an entire district. Managers who begin as technicians gain experience that affords them special skills and judgment.

Self-employment also offers interesting and lucrative opportunities. For example, because many drilling rigs are owned by small, private owners, technicians can become independent owners and operators of drilling rigs. The rewards for successfully operating an independent drill can be very great, especially if the owner discovers new fields and shares in the royalties for production.

Working as a consultant or a technical salesperson can lead to advancement in the petroleum industry. Success is contingent upon an excellent record of field success in oil and gas drilling and production.

In some areas, advancement requires further education. Well loggers who want to analyze logs are required to have at least a bachelor's degree in geology or petroleum engineering, and sometimes they need a master's degree. With additional schooling and a bachelor's degree, an engineering technician can become an engineer. For advanced level engineering, a master's degree is the minimum requirement and a doctorate is typically required. Upper-level researchers also need a doctorate.

EARNINGS

Because of their many work situations and conditions, petroleum technicians' salaries vary widely. Salaries also vary according to geographic location, experience, and education. Petroleum and geological technicians had median annual earnings of $54,020 in 2010, according to the U.S. Department of Labor (DOL). Salaries ranged from less than $29,950 to $99,860 or more annually.

In general, technicians working in remote areas and under severe weather conditions usually receive higher rates of pay, as do technicians who work at major oil companies and companies with unions.

Fringe benefits are good. Most employers provide health and accident insurance, sick pay, retirement plans, profit-sharing plans, and paid vacations. Education benefits are also competitive.

WORK ENVIRONMENT

Petroleum technicians' workplaces and conditions vary as widely as their duties. They may work on land or offshore, at drilling sites or in laboratories, in offices, or refineries.

Field technicians do their work outdoors, day and night, in all kinds of weather. Drilling and production crews work all over the world, often in swamps, deserts, or in the mountains. The work is rugged and physical, and more dangerous than many other kinds of work. Safety is a big concern. Workers are subject to falls and other accidents on rigs, and blowouts can injure or kill workers if well pressure is not controlled.

Drilling crews often move from place to place because work in a particular field may be completed in a few weeks or months. Technicians who work on production wells usually remain in the same location for long periods. Hours are often long for both groups of workers.

Those working on offshore rigs and platforms can experience strong ocean currents, tides, and storms. Living quarters are usually small, like those on a ship, but they are adequate and comfortable. Workers generally live and work on the drilling platform for days at a time and then get several days off away from the rig, returning to shore by helicopter or crewboat.

Engineering technicians generally work indoors in clean, well-lit offices, although some may also spend part of their time in the field. Regular, 40-hour workweeks are the norm, although some may occasionally work irregular hours.

OUTLOOK

Little or no employment change is expected for petroleum technicians through 2018, according to the DOL. The employment outlook for petroleum technicians is closely linked to the price of oil. When the price of oil is low, companies often reduce exploration and, consequently, the number of technicians needed. When the price of oil is high, more exploration is conducted, and there are more opportunities for technicians.

Besides looking for new fields, companies are also expending much effort to boost production in existing fields. New cost-effective technology that permits new drilling and increases production will continue to be important in helping the profitability of the oil industry.

The oil industry plays an important role in the economy and employment. Oil and gas will continue to be primary energy sources for many decades. Most job openings will be due to retirements and job transfer. Technicians with specialized training will have the best employment opportunities. The DOL reports that professional, scientific, and technical services firms will increasingly seek the services of petroleum technicians who can act as consultants regarding environmental policy and federal pollution mandates.

FOR MORE INFORMATION

Visit the association's Web site for information on careers and membership for college students, as well as answers to frequently asked questions about the field.

American Association of Petroleum Geologists
PO Box 979
Tulsa, OK 74101-0979
Tel: 800-364-2274
http://www.aapg.org

The institute represents the professional interests of oil and natural gas companies. Visit its Web site for career information and facts and statistics about the petroleum industry.

American Petroleum Institute
1220 L Street, NW
Washington, DC 20005-4070
Tel: 202-682-8000
http://www.api.org

For information about JETS programs, products, and engineering career brochures (in many disciplines), contact

Junior Engineering Technical Society (JETS)
1420 King Street, Suite 405
Alexandria, VA 22314-2750
Tel: 703-548-5387
E-mail: info@jets.org
http://www.jets.org

For a list of petroleum technology schools and information on careers in petroleum engineering, contact

Society of Petroleum Engineers
222 Palisades Creek Drive
Richardson, TX 75080-2040
Tel: 800-456-6863
E-mail: spedal@spe.org
http://www.spe.org

For a training catalog listing publications, audiovisuals, and short courses, including correspondence courses, contact
University of Texas at Austin
Petroleum Extension Service
One University Station, R8100
Austin, TX 78712-1100
Tel: 800-687-4132
E-mail: petex@www.utexas.edu
http://www.utexas.edu/cee/petex

Petrologists

OVERVIEW

Geologists study the overall formation of the earth and its history, the movements of the earth's crust, and its mineral compositions and other natural resources. *Petrologists* focus specifically upon the analysis of the composition, structure, and history of rocks and rock formations. Petrologists are also interested in the formation of particular types of rocks that contain economically important materials such as gold, copper, and uranium. They also study the formation and composition of metals, precious stones, minerals, and meteorites, and they analyze a wide variety of substances, ranging from diamonds and gold to petroleum deposits that may be locked in rock formations beneath the earth's surface.

HISTORY

The field of petrology began to emerge in the early part of the 20th century as a subspecialty within geology. During this period, the mining of oil, coal, precious metals, uranium, and other substances increased rapidly. With the development of the gasoline engine in the mid-1950s, oil became the most significant raw material produced in the world, and the study of the earth's rock formations became invaluable to the mining of petroleum. In fact, the petroleum industry is the largest employer of petrologists; most are employed by one segment or another of the mining industry. Petrologists are also used in many other areas of mining and mineral extraction, and they are employed by numerous government agencies.

Common Minerals and Their Uses

Aluminum
Uses: transportation, packaging, building, electrical, machinery

Feldspar
Uses: glass and ceramics, fertilizer, insulation

Gold
Uses: jewelry, dentistry/medicine, scientific and electronic instruments

Quartz
Uses: glass, paints, precision instruments

Rare Earth Elements
Uses: hybrid vehicles (batteries), metallurgical additives, ceramics and polishing compounds

Silica
Uses: computer chips, ceramics, water filtration systems

Uranium
Uses: nuclear power generation

Zinc
Uses: agricultural, chemicals, rubber production

Sources: *Facts About Minerals*, National Mining Association; Mineral Information Institute, U.S. Geological Survey

THE JOB

The major goal of petrology is to study the origin, composition, and history of rocks and rock formations. Because petrologists are intimately involved in the mining industry, they may work closely with the following types of scientists: geologists, who study the overall composition and structure of the earth as well as mineral deposits; *geophysicists*, who study the physical movements of the earth including seismic activity and physical properties of the earth and its atmosphere; *hydrologists*, who study the earth's waters and water systems; *mineralogists*, who examine and classify minerals and precious stones; and *paleontologists*, who study the fossilized remains of plants and animals found in geological formations.

Depending upon the type of work they do, petrologists may frequently work in teams with scientists from other specialties.

For example, in oil drilling they may work with geologists and geophysicists. The petrologist is responsible for analyzing rocks from bored samples beneath the earth's surface to determine the oil-bearing composition of rock samples as well as to determine whether certain rock formations are likely to have oil or natural gas content. In precious metal mining operations, petrologists may work closely with mineralogists. They may analyze core samples of mineral rock formations, called mineral ore, while the mineralogists analyze in detail the specific mineral or minerals contained in such samples.

Because the surface of the earth is composed of thousands of layers of rock formations shaped over several billion years, the contents of these layers can be revealing, depending upon the rock and mineral composition of each respective layer. Each layer, or stratum, of rock beneath the earth's surface tells a story of the earth's condition in the past and can reveal characteristics such as weather patterns, temperatures, flow of water, movement of glaciers, volcanic activity, and numerous other characteristics. These layers can also reveal the presence of minerals, mineral ores, and extractable fossil fuels such as petroleum and natural gas.

Petrologists spend time both in the field gathering samples and in the laboratory analyzing those samples. They use physical samples, photographs, maps, and diagrams to describe the characteristics of whatever formations they are analyzing. They use chemical compounds to break down rocks and rock materials to isolate certain elements. They use X-rays, spectroscopic examination, electron microscopes, and other sophisticated means of testing and analyzing samples to isolate the specific components of various minerals and elements within the samples in order to draw conclusions from their analyses.

REQUIREMENTS

High School

If you are interested in a career in petrology, you should be aware that you will need an extensive education. Begin preparing yourself for this education by taking college prep courses while in high school. It will be important to focus your studies on the sciences, such as earth science, biology, chemistry, and physics, and on mathematics, including algebra, geometry, and calculus. You should also take speech and English classes to hone your research, writing, and speaking skills. In addition, take computer science, geography, and history classes.

Postsecondary Training

Most professional positions in the field of petrology require a master's degree or a doctorate. Although individuals without these degrees can technically become petrologists, advances in the field and the profession's requirements will make it extremely difficult to enter the field without a graduate degree.

In college, you should concentrate your studies on the earth and physical sciences, geology, paleontology, mineralogy, and, of course, physics, chemistry, and mathematics. Because petrologists frequently analyze large volumes of data and write reports on such data, courses in computer science and English composition are advisable. Many students begin their careers in petrology by first majoring in geology or paleontology as an undergraduate and then, as graduate students, enter formal training in the field of petrology.

The two major professional associations that provide information and continuing education to petrologists are the Geological Society of America and the American Association of Petroleum Geologists. The American Geological Institute GEO Directory (http://www.agiweb.org/workforce/dgd) provides a list of colleges and universities that offer formal training in this area.

Certification or Licensing

Although no special certification exists for the field of petrology, several states require the registration of petrologists, and government petrologists may be required to take the civil service examination.

Other Requirements

Requirements for this profession depend in large part upon the segment or subspecialty of the profession you choose. In some cases, petrologists work within a confined geographic area and spend most of their time in laboratories. In other instances, petrologists are called upon to travel throughout the United States and even overseas. Extensive travel is often required if you are working for a multinational oil company or other mining operation where you need to be available on short notice to analyze samples in various localities. Where important mining operations are undertaken, petrologists may be required to analyze rocks, ore, core samples, or other materials on short notice and under deadline pressure.

As with other scientific disciplines, teamwork is often an essential part of the job. Petrologists must be able to understand and relate to geologists, paleontologists, mineralogists, and other scientific experts; they must also be able to relate to and communicate their findings to supervisory personnel who may lack a strong technical background.

If you are considering petrology, you must be able to work well with others, as well as independently, on various projects. You should also enjoy travel and the outdoors.

EXPLORING

To explore your interest in this field, join your school's science club and any local rock-hunting groups to become actively involved in science. Talk to your science teachers about petrology; they may know of a petrologist you can interview to find out about his or her experiences and education. Your high school counselor may also be able to help you arrange such an information interview. Petrologists may be found in universities and colleges that offer courses in geology and petrology, in certain government offices and field offices, and especially throughout the mining, oil, and natural gas industries.

Both geologists and petrologists require assistance in their work, and it is possible to obtain summer jobs and part-time employment in certain parts of the country where mining or oil exploration activities are taking place. If such work is unavailable to you, try to get a part-time or summer job at a museum in your area that has a geology department, rock collections, or mineral collections. Volunteering at museums is also possible.

For further information about the field of petrology and about various conferences in the geological professions, contact the organizations listed at the end of this article.

EMPLOYERS

Because much of the practice of petrology relates to the extraction of minerals, fossil fuels, metals, and natural resources, most petrologists work for petroleum and mining companies. Their work includes mining on the earth's surface, beneath the earth's surface, and under the ocean floor (in the case of offshore oil drilling, for example). Other petrologists work for federal, state, and local governments. In the federal branch, petrologists are often employed by the Environmental Protection Agency, the Department of Agriculture, the Department of Energy, the Department of Defense, the Department of Commerce, and the Department of the Interior. In fact, the largest government employer is the U.S. Geological Survey, a branch of the U.S. Department of the Interior. Other petrologists teach earth science in high schools, teach geology and petrology courses in colleges and universities, or work as consultants.

The field of petrology consists of a number of activities and sub-specialties, and during their careers petrologists normally specialize in one area.

STARTING OUT

Both the federal government and state governments employ petrologists in various agencies. Thus, if you are undertaking graduate programs in petrology, you should contact both state civil service agencies in your respective state and the federal Office of Personnel Management (OPM). Federal agencies generally notify the OPM when they wish to fill vacancies in various positions and when new positions are created. The OPM has job information centers located in major cities throughout the United States, as well as a Web site, http://www.usajobs.opm.gov, that lists job openings. You can also obtain job information through employment offices in your state.

Although industrial firms do engage in campus recruiting, particularly for master's and doctoral level job applicants, less recruiting is occurring now than in the past. Thus, job seekers should not hesitate to contact oil exploration companies, mining companies, and other organizations directly. It is always a good idea to contact geologists and petrologists directly in various companies to learn about opportunities.

Part-time employment is available to geologists and petrologists in both private industry and various federal and state agencies. In some cases, agencies use volunteer students and scientists and pay only some expenses rather than a full salary. This arrangement may still be a good way to gain experience and to meet professionals in the field.

If you wish to teach petrology, you should consult college and university employment listings. For graduate students in the field, a limited number of part-time jobs, as well as instructor-level jobs, are available.

Note that junior high schools and high schools generally need more instructors in the earth sciences than do colleges. This new reality reflects the fact that many high schools are beginning to offer a broader range of science courses. Individuals with a master's or doctoral degree are likely to be qualified to teach a variety of courses at the high school level, including earth science, physics, chemistry, mathematics, and biology.

ADVANCEMENT

Because the level of competition in this field is keen and the oil industry is subject to fluctuation, those wishing to enter the petrology profession must think seriously about obtaining the highest level of education possible.

Advancement in the field generally involves spending a number of years as a staff scientist and then taking on supervisory and managerial responsibilities. The abilities to work on a team, to perform accurate and timely research, and to take charge of projects are all important for advancement in this field.

Because petrology, geology, and mineralogy are sciences that overlap, especially in industry, it is possible for petrologists to become mineralogists or geologists under the right circumstances. The fact that the three disciplines are intimately related can work to a person's advantage, particularly in changing economic times.

EARNINGS

Earnings for petrologists vary according to a person's educational attainment, experience, and ability. A salary survey from the American Association of Petroleum Geologists found that in 2009 petroleum geologists with bachelor's degrees and three to five years of work experience had average salaries of $99,800; with 10–14 years of experience, $110,300; and 25+ years of experience, $189,900. The U.S. Department of Labor (DOL) reports that the median annual salary for geoscientists, except hydrologists and geographers, was $82,500 in 2010. The lowest paid 10 percent earned less than $43,820, while the highest paid 10 percent earned more than $160,910. Geoscientists earned the following mean annual earnings by employer: oil and gas extraction, $132,210; federal government, $95,580; and state government, $62,880.

Petrologists employed by oil companies or consulting firms generally start at somewhat higher salaries than those who work for the government, but private industry favors those with master's or doctoral degrees.

Many petrologists are eligible to receive fringe benefits, such as life and health insurance, paid vacations, and pension plans.

WORK ENVIRONMENT

Because the field of petrology involves a considerable amount of testing of rocks, ores, and other materials at mining sites and other types of geological sites, petrologists can expect to travel a considerable amount. In some cases, petrologists must travel back and forth from a field site to a laboratory several times while conducting a series of tests. If petrologists are working on exploratory investigations of a potential site for fuel, they may be at a remote location for weeks or months, until the data collected are sufficient to return to the laboratory. The conditions may be arduous, and there may be little to do during leisure time.

The hours and working conditions of petrologists vary, but petrologists working in the field can generally expect long hours. Petrologists, geologists, and mineralogists frequently work in teams, and petrologists may work under the supervision of a head geologist, for example. In private industry, they also frequently work with mining engineers, mine supervisors, drilling supervisors, and others who are all part of a larger mining or drilling operation.

OUTLOOK

The DOL reports that employment opportunities for geoscientists will grow faster than the average for all occupations through 2018. Opportunities for petrologists—especially those who are employed by the oil and gas industries and consulting firms—will be good. Rising demand for oil throughout the world has spurred an increase in oil drilling and exploration. As a result, the number of new jobs in this field has increased, and the number of students who graduate with degrees in petrology or geology is on the rise. Additionally, environmental regulations will create a need for these scientists in environmental protection and reclamation work. Those with master's degrees, who speak a foreign language, and who are willing to travel abroad for employment will have the best employment prospects.

FOR MORE INFORMATION

Visit the association's Web site for information on careers and membership for college students, as well as answers to frequently asked questions about the field.
American Association of Petroleum Geologists
PO Box 979
Tulsa, OK 74101-0979
Tel: 800-364-2274
http://www.aapg.org

For information on careers, contact
American Geological Institute
4220 King Street
Alexandria, VA 22302-1502

Tel: 703-379-2480
http://www.agiweb.org

For career information, contact
Association of Environmental and Engineering Geologists
PO Box 460518
Denver, CO 80246-0518
Tel: 303-757-2926
E-mail: aeg@aegweb.org
http://aegweb.org

For information on internships, contact
Geological Society of America
PO Box 9140
Boulder, CO 80301-9140
Tel: 888-443-4472
E-mail: gsaservice@geosociety.org
http://www.geosociety.org

The society is a membership organization for "scientists and engineers involved with coal petrology, kerogen petrology, organic geochemistry and related disciplines." Visit its Web site for more information.
Society for Organic Petrology
E-mail: info@tsop.org
http://tsop.org

Science Writers and Editors

QUICK FACTS

School Subjects
Earth science
English

Personal Skills
Communication/ideas
Technical/scientific

Work Environment
Indoors and outdoors
Primarily multiple locations

Minimum Education Level
Bachelor's degree

Salary Range
$28,610 to $55,240 to
$109,440+ (writers)
$28,880 to $51,470 to
$96,800 (editors)

Certification or Licensing
None available

Outlook
About as fast as the average

DOT
131, 132

GOE
01.02.01

NOC
5121, 5122

O*NET-SOC
27-3041.00, 27-3042.00,
27-3043.00

OVERVIEW

Science writers translate technical scientific information so it can be disseminated to the general public and professionals in the field. They research, interpret, write, and edit scientific information. Their work often appears in books, technical studies and reports, magazine and trade journal articles, newspapers, company newsletters, and on Web sites and may be used for radio and television broadcasts. Other science writers work as *public information officers* for government science agencies and museums and other organizations.

Science editors perform a wide range of functions, but their primary responsibility is to ensure that text provided by science writers is suitable in content, format, and style for the intended audiences. Readers are an editor's first priority.

HISTORY

The skill of writing has existed for thousands of years. Papyrus fragments with writing by ancient Egyptians date from about 3000 B.C., and archaeological findings show that the Chinese had developed books by about 1300 B.C.

The history of book editing is tied closely to the history of the book and bookmaking and the history of the printing process. In the early days of publishing, authors worked directly with the printer, and the printer was often the publisher and seller of the author's work. Eventually, however, booksellers began to work directly with the authors and eventually took over the role of publisher. The publisher then became the middleman between author and printer. The publisher worked closely with the author and sometimes acted as the editor; the word *editor*, in fact, derives from the Latin word *edere* or *editum* and means supervising or directing the preparation of text. Eventually, specialists were hired to perform the editing function. These editors, who were also called advisers or literary advisers in the 19th century, became an integral part of the publishing business.

The editor, also called the sponsor in some houses, sought out the best authors, worked with them, and became their advocate in the publishing house. So important did some editors become that their very presence in a publishing house could determine the quality of author that might be published there. The field has grown through the 20th and 21st century, with computers greatly speeding up the process by which editors prepare text for the printer or electronic publication.

The broadcasting industry has also contributed to the development of the professional writer. Film, radio, and television are sources of entertainment, information, and education that provide employment for thousands of writers. Today, the computer industry and Internet Web sites have also created the need for more writers.

As our world becomes more complex and people seek even more information, professional writers have become increasingly important. And, as science takes giant steps forward and discoveries are being made every day that impact our lives, skilled science writers are needed to document these changes and disseminate the information to the general public and more specialized audiences.

THE JOB

Science writers usually write for the general public. They translate scientific information into articles and reports that the general public and the media can understand. They might write about the causes and effects of volcanoes, the discovery of rare fossils during a construction dig, new developments in earthquake detection research, and countless other topics. Good writers who cover the subjects thoroughly have inquisitive minds and enjoy looking for additional information that might add to their articles. They research the topic to gain a thorough understanding of the subject matter. This may require hours of research on the Internet; in corporate, university, or public libraries; at science facilities; or out in the natural world. Writers always need good background information regarding a subject before they can write about it.

In order to get the information required, writers may interview scientists (such as geologists, geophysicists, hydrologists, soil scientists, etc.), politicians, college professors, and others who are familiar with the subject. Writers must know how to present the information so it can be understood. This requires knowing the audience and how to reach them. For example, an article on volcanoes may need graphs, photos, or historical facts. Writers sometimes enlist the help of graphic designers in order to add a visual dimension to their work.

For example, if reporting on earthquakes, writers will need to illustrate the geological factors that cause an earthquake. The public will also want to know what areas of the United States are at risk for earthquakes, what government agencies are doing to prepare their citizens for future earthquakes, and other information. In addition, interviews with geophysicists and earthquake survivors add a personal touch to the story.

Writers usually need to work quickly because news-related stories are often deadline-oriented. Because science can be so complex, science writers also need to help the audience understand and evaluate the information. Writing for the Web encompasses most journalistic guidelines including time constraints and sometimes space constraints.

Some science writers specialize in their subject matter. For instance, a science writer may write only about dinosaurs and earn a reputation as the best writer in that subject area.

Some writers may choose to be freelance writers either on a full- or part-time basis, or to supplement other jobs. Freelance science writers are self-employed writers who work with small and large companies, research institutions, or publishing firms on a contract or hourly basis. They may specialize in writing about a specific scientific subject for one or two clients, or they may write about a broad range of subjects for a number of different clients. Many freelance writers write articles, papers, or reports and then attempt to get them published in newspapers, trade, or consumer publications.

Editors work for many kinds of publishers, publications, and corporations. Editors' titles vary widely, not only from one area of publishing to another but also within each area. *Book editors* prepare written material for publication. In small publishing houses, the same editor may guide the material through all the stages of the publishing process. They may work with printers, designers, advertising agencies, and other members of the publishing industry. In larger publishing houses, editors tend to be more specialized, being involved in only a part of the publishing process. *Acquisitions editors* are the editors who find new writers and sign on new projects. They find new ideas for books that will sell well and find writers who can create the books.

Production editors take the manuscript written by an author and polish the work into a finished print or electronic publication. They correct grammar, spelling, and style, and check all the facts. They make sure the book reads well and suggest changes to the author if it does not. The production editor may be responsible for getting the cover designed and the art put into a book. Because the work is so demanding, production editors usually work on only one or two books at a time.

Copy editors assist the production editor in polishing the author's writing. Copy editors review each page and make all the changes required to give the book a good writing style. *Line editors* review the text to make sure specific style rules are obeyed. They make sure the same spelling is used for words where more than one spelling is correct (for example, grey and gray).

Fact checkers and *proofreaders* read the manuscript to make sure everything is spelled correctly and that all the facts in the text have been checked.

The basic functions performed by *magazine* and *newspaper editors* are much like those performed by book editors, but a significant amount of the writing that appears in magazines and newspapers, or periodicals, is done by *staff writers*. Periodicals often use editors who specialize in specific areas, such as *city editors*, who oversee the work of reporters who specialize in local news, and *department editors*. Department editors specialize in areas such as business, fashion, sports, and features, to name only a few. These departments are determined by the interests of the audience that the periodical intends to reach. Like book houses, periodicals use copy editors, researchers, and fact checkers, but at small periodicals, one or a few editors may be responsible for tasks that would be performed by many people at a larger publication.

REQUIREMENTS
High School

If you are considering a career as a writer or editor, you should take English, journalism, and communication courses in high school. Computer classes will also be helpful. If you know in high school that you want to do scientific writing or editing, it would be to your advantage to take biology, physiology, earth science, chemistry, physics, math, and other science-related courses. If your school offers journalism courses and you have the chance to work on the school newspaper or yearbook, you should take advantage of these opportunities. Part-time employment at newspapers, publishing companies, or scientific research facilities can also provide experience and insight regarding this career.

Postsecondary Training

Although not all writers and editors are college-educated, today's jobs almost always require a bachelor's degree. Many writers earn an undergraduate degree in English, journalism, or liberal arts and then obtain a master's degree in a communications field such as writing. A good liberal arts education is important since you are often required to write about many subject areas. Earth science-related courses (or even pursuing a science-related field, such as geology, geophysics, soil science, or environmental science, as a second major) are highly recommended. You should investigate internship programs that give you experience in the communications department of a corporation, environmental firm, government science agency, or research facility. Some newspapers, magazines, or public relations firms also have internships that give you the opportunity to write and work as an editor.

Some people find that after working as a writer, their interests are strong in a science field and they evolve into that writing specialty. They may return to school and enter a master's degree program or take some additional courses related specifically to science writing. Similarly, science majors may find that they like the writing aspect of their jobs and return to school to pursue a career as a science writer.

Other Requirements

Writers and editors should be creative and able to express ideas clearly, have an interest in science, be skilled in research techniques, and be computer literate. Other assets include curiosity, persistence, initiative, resourcefulness, and an accurate memory. For some jobs—on a newspaper, for example, where the activity is hectic and deadlines short—the ability to concentrate and produce under pressure is essential.

You must be detail oriented to succeed as a writer or an editor. You must also be patient, since you may have to spend hours synthesizing information into the written or electronic word or turning a few pages of near-gibberish into powerful, elegant English. If you are the kind of person who can't sit still, you probably will not succeed in these careers. To be a good writer or editor, you must be a self-starter who is not afraid to make decisions. You must be good not only at identifying problems but also at solving them, so you must be creative.

EXPLORING

As a high school or college student, you can test your interest and aptitude in the field of writing and editing by serving as a reporter or writer on school newspapers, yearbooks, and literary magazines. Attending writing workshops and taking writing classes will give you the opportunity to practice and sharpen your skills. Practice editing your own work or the work of friends to get a basic introduction of what it takes to work as an editor.

Community newspapers often welcome contributions from outside sources, although they may not have the resources to pay for them. Jobs in bookstores, magazine shops, libraries, and even newsstands offer a chance to become familiar with various publications. If you are interested in science writing or editing, try to get a part-time job in a research laboratory, interview science writers and editors, and read good science writing in major newspapers such as the *New York Times* or in publications published by major science associations.

Information on writing as a career may also be obtained by visiting local newspapers and publishing houses and interviewing some of the writers and editors who work there. Career conferences and other guidance programs frequently include speakers from local or national organizations who can provide information on communication careers.

Some professional organizations such as the Society for Technical Communication welcome students as members and have special student membership rates and career information. In addition, participation in professional organizations gives you the opportunity to meet and visit with people in this career field.

EMPLOYERS

Many science writers and editors are employed, often on a freelance basis, by newspaper, magazine, and book publishers, and the broadcast industries as well. Internet publishing is a growing field that hires science writers and editors. Science writers and editors are also employed by scientific research companies; government agencies that conduct scientific research and other federal, state, and local government agencies; and research and development departments of corporations. Large colleges and universities often employ science writers and editors in their public relations departments and as writing professors. Zoos, aquariums, museums, and government agencies also employ writers as public information officers.

STARTING OUT

A fair amount of experience is required to gain a high-level position in this field. Most writers start out in entry-level positions. These jobs may be listed with college career services offices, or you may apply directly to the employment departments of publishing companies, corporations, institutions, universities, research facilities, nonprofit organizations, and government facilities that hire science writers. Many firms now hire writers directly upon application or recommendation of college professors and career services offices. Want ads in newspapers and trade journals are another source for jobs. Serving an internship in college can give you the advantage of knowing people who can give you personal recommendations.

Internships are also excellent ways to build your portfolio. Employers in the communications field are usually interested in seeing samples of your published writing assembled in an organized portfolio or scrapbook. Working on your college's magazine or newspaper staff can help you build a portfolio. Sometimes small, regional or local magazines and newspapers will also buy articles or assign short pieces for you to write. You should attempt to build your portfolio with good writing samples. Be sure to include the type of writing you are interested in doing, if possible.

You may need to begin your career as a junior writer or editor and work your way up. This usually involves library research, preparation of rough drafts for part or all of a report, cataloging, and other related writing tasks. These are generally carried on under the supervision of a senior writer.

Many science writers enter the field after working in public relations departments or science-related industries. They may use their skills to transfer to specialized writing positions or they may take additional courses or graduate work that focuses on writing or documentation skills.

There is tremendous competition for editorial jobs, so it is important for a beginner who wishes to break into the business to be as well prepared as possible. College students who have gained experience as interns, have worked for publications during summer vacations, or have attended special programs in publishing will be at an advantage. In addition, applicants for any editorial position must be extremely careful when preparing cover letters and resumes. Even a single error in spelling or usage will disqualify an applicant. Applicants for editorial or proofreading positions must also expect to take and pass tests that are designed to determine their language skills.

Many editors enter the field as editorial assistants or proofreaders. Some editorial assistants perform only clerical tasks, whereas others may also proofread or perform basic editorial tasks. Typically, an editorial assistant who performs well will be given the opportunity to take on more and more editorial duties as time passes. Proofreaders have the advantage of being able to look at the work of editors, so they can learn while they do their own work.

Good sources of information about job openings are school career services offices, classified ads in newspapers and trade journals, specialized publications such as *Publishers Weekly* (http://www .publishersweekly.com), and Web sites. One way to proceed is to identify local publishers through the Yellow Pages. Many publishers have Web sites that list job openings, and large publishers often have telephone job lines that serve the same purpose.

ADVANCEMENT

Writers with only an undergraduate degree may choose to earn a graduate degree in science writing, corporate communications, graphic design, or a related program. An advanced degree may open doors to more progressive career options.

Many experienced science writers are often promoted to head writing, documentation, or public relations departments within corporations or institutions. Some may become recognized experts in their field and their writings may be in demand by trade journals, newspapers, magazines, and the broadcast industry. Writers employed by newspapers and magazines may advance by working for larger, more prestigious publications.

As freelance writers prove themselves and work successfully with clients, they may be able to demand increased contract fees or hourly rates.

In book publishing houses, employees who start as editorial assistants or proofreaders and show promise generally become copy editors. After gaining skill in that position, they may be given a wider range of duties while retaining the same title. The next step may be a position as a *senior copy editor*, which involves overseeing the work of junior copy editors, or as a project editor. The *project editor* performs a wide variety of tasks, including copyediting, coordinating the work of in-house and freelance copy editors, and managing the schedule of a particular project. From this position, an editor may move up to become *first assistant editor*, then *managing editor*, then *editor-in-chief*. These positions involve more management and decision making than is usually found in the positions described previously. The editor-in-chief works with the publisher to ensure that a suitable editorial policy is being followed, while the managing editor is responsible for all aspects of the editorial department. The assistant editor provides support to the managing editor.

Newspaper editors generally begin working on the copy desk, where they progress from less significant stories and projects to major news and feature stories. A common route to advancement is for copy editors to be promoted to a particular department, where they may move up the ranks to management positions. An editor who has achieved success in a department may become a city editor, who is responsible for news, or a managing editor, who runs the entire editorial operation of a newspaper.

The advancement path for magazine editors is similar to that of book editors. After they become copy editors, they work their way up to become senior editors, managing editors, and editors-in-chief. In many cases, magazine editors advance by moving from a position on one magazine to the same position with a larger or more prestigious magazine. Such moves often bring significant increases in both pay and status.

EARNINGS

Although there are no specific salary surveys for science writers, salary information for all writers is available. The U.S. Department of Labor (DOL) reports that the median annual salary for writers was $55,240 in 2010. Salaries ranged from less than $28,610 to more than $109,440. Mean annual earnings for writers employed by newspaper, book, and directory publishers were $56,210 in 2010. Technical writers earned salaries that ranged from less than $37,160 to $100,910 or more.

The DOL reports that the median annual earnings for all editors were $51,470 in 2010. Salaries ranged from $28,880 or less to more than $96,800. Those who worked for newspaper, periodical, book, and directory publishers earned annual mean salaries of $58,270.

Freelance writers' and editors' earnings can vary depending on their expertise, reputation, and the articles they are contracted to write.

Most full-time writing and editing positions offer the usual benefits such as insurance, sick leave, and paid vacation. Some jobs also provide tuition reimbursement and retirement benefits. Freelance writers must pay for their own insurance. However, there are professional associations that may offer group insurance rates for their members.

WORK ENVIRONMENT

Work environment depends on the type of science writing and the employer. Generally, writers work in an office or research environment. Writers for the news media sometimes work in noisy surroundings. Some writers travel to research information and conduct interviews while other employers may confine research to local libraries or the Internet. In addition, some employers require writers to conduct research interviews over the phone, rather than in person.

Although the workweek usually runs 35 to 40 hours in a normal office setting, many writers may have to work overtime to cover a story, interview people, meet deadlines, or to disseminate information in a timely manner. The newspaper and broadcasting industries deliver the news 24 hours a day, seven days a week. Writers often work nights and weekends to meet press deadlines or to cover a late-developing story.

Each day may bring new and interesting situations. Some stories may even take writers to remote and exotic locales. Other assignments may be boring or they may take place in less than desirable settings, where interview subjects may be rude, busy, and unwilling to talk or conditions may be cold, snowy, rainy, or otherwise uncomfortable. One of the most difficult elements for writers may be meeting deadlines or gathering information. People who are the most content as writers work well with deadline pressure.

The environments in which editors work vary widely. For the most part, publishers of all kinds realize that a quiet atmosphere is conducive to work that requires tremendous concentration. It takes an unusual ability to focus to edit in a noisy place. Most editors work in private offices or cubicles. Book editors often work in quieter surroundings than do newspaper editors or quality-control people in advertising agencies, who sometimes work in rather loud and hectic situations.

Even in relatively quiet surroundings, however, editors often have many distractions. A project editor who is trying to do some copyediting or review the editing of others may, for example, have to deal with phone calls from authors, questions from junior editors, meetings with members of the editorial and production staff, and questions from freelancers, among many other distractions.

Deadlines are an important issue for virtually all editors. Newspaper and magazine editors work in a much more pressurized atmosphere than book editors because they face daily or weekly deadlines, whereas book production usually takes place over several months.

In almost all cases, editors must work long hours during certain phases of the editing process. Some newspaper editors start work at

5 A.M., others work until 11 P.M. or even through the night. Feature editors, columnists, and editorial page editors usually can schedule their day in a more regular fashion, as can editors who work on weekly newspapers. Editors working on hard news, however, may receive an assignment that must be completed, even if work extends well into the next shift.

OUTLOOK

According to the DOL, there is strong competition for writing and editing jobs, and growth in writing careers should occur at an average rate through 2018. Opportunities will be good for science writers, as continued developments in the field will drive the need for skilled writers to put complex scientific information in terms that a wide and varied audience can understand.

FOR MORE INFORMATION

The ACES is an excellent source of information about careers in copyediting. It organizes educational seminars and maintains lists of internships.
American Copy Editors Society (ACES)
http://www.copydesk.org

The ASNE helps editors maintain the highest standards of quality, improve their craft, and better serve their communities. It preserves and promotes core journalistic values. Visit its Web site to read online publications such as Why Choose Journalism? *and* Preparing for a Career in Newspapers.
American Society of News Editors (ASNE)
11690B Sunrise Valley Drive
Reston, VA 20191-1436
Tel: 703-453-1122
E-mail: asne@asne.org
http://www.asne.org

For information on membership, contact
Association of Earth Science Editors
http://www.aese.org

For information on careers in science writing, contact
Council for the Advancement of Science Writing
PO Box 910
Hedgesville, WV 25427-0910

Tel: 304-754-6786
http://www.casw.org

To read advice for beginning science writers, visit the NASW Web site.
National Association of Science Writers (NASW)
PO Box 7905
Berkeley, CA 94707-0905
Tel: 510-647-9500
http://www.nasw.org

For information about working as a writer and union membership,
contact
National Writers Union
256 West 38th Street, Suite 703
New York, NY 10018-9807
Tel: 212-254-0279
http://www.nwu.org

For information on scholarships and student memberships aimed
at those preparing for a career in technical communication, contact
Society for Technical Communication
9401 Lee Highway, Suite 300
Fairfax, VA 22031-1803
Tel: 703-522-4114
E-mail: stc@src.org
http://www.stc.org

For a wide range of resources relating to environmental journalism,
contact
Society of Environmental Journalists
PO Box 2492
Jenkintown, PA 19046-8492
Tel: 215-884-8174
E-mail: sej@sej.org
http://www.sej.org

This organization for journalists has campus and online chapters.
Society of Professional Journalists
Eugene S. Pulliam National Journalism Center
3909 North Meridian Street
Indianapolis, IN 46208-4011
Tel: 317-927-8000
http://www.spj.org

Soil Scientists

QUICK FACTS

School Subjects
Agriculture
Earth science

Personal Skills
Leadership/management
Technical/scientific

Work Environment
Indoors and outdoors
Primarily multiple locations

Minimum Education Level
Bachelor's degree

Salary Range
$34,420 to $57,340 to
$120,000

Certification or Licensing
Voluntary

Outlook
Faster than the average

DOT
040

GOE
02.03.02

NOC
2115

O*NET-SOC
19-1013.00

OVERVIEW

Soil scientists study the physical, chemical, and biological characteristics of soils to determine the most productive and effective planting strategies. Their research aids in producing larger, healthier crops and more environmentally sound farming procedures. There are about 13,900 soil and plant scientists in the United States.

HISTORY

Hundreds of years ago, farmers planted crops without restriction; they were unaware that soil could be depleted of necessary nutrients by overuse. When crops were poor, farmers often blamed the weather instead of their farming techniques.

Soil, one of our most important natural resources, was taken for granted until its condition became too bad to ignore. An increasing population, moreover, made the United States aware that its own welfare depends on fertile soil capable of producing food for hundreds of millions of people.

Increasing concerns about feeding a growing nation brought agricultural practices into reevaluation. In 1862, the U.S. Department of Agriculture (USDA) was created to give farmers information about new crops and improved farming techniques. Although the department started small, today the USDA is one of the largest agencies of the federal government.

Following the creation of the USDA, laws were created to further promote and protect farmers. The 1933 Agricultural Adjustment Act inaugurated a policy of giving direct government aid to farmers. Two years later, the Natural Resources Conservation Service was

A soil scientist (right) and a geologist study a soil core sediment sample. (*Jim Craven, AP Photo*/Medford Mail Tribune)

created after disastrous dust storms blew away millions of tons of valuable topsoil and destroyed fertile cropland throughout parts of Oklahoma, Texas, Kansas, New Mexico, and Colorado.

Since 1937, states have organized themselves into soil conservation districts. Each local division coordinates with the USDA, assigning soil scientists and soil conservationists to help local farmers establish and maintain farming practices that will use land in the wisest possible ways.

THE JOB

Soil is formed by the breaking of rocks and the decay of trees, plants, and animals. It may take as long as 500 years to make just one inch of topsoil. Unwise and wasteful farming methods can destroy that inch of soil in just a few short years. In addition, rainstorms may carry thousands of pounds of precious topsoil away and dissolve chemicals that are necessary to grow healthy crops through a process called erosion. Soil scientists work with engineers to address these issues.

Soil scientists spend much of their time outdoors, investigating fields, advising farmers about crop rotation or fertilizers, assessing field drainage, and taking soil samples. After researching an area, they may suggest certain crops to farmers to protect bare earth from the ravages of the wind and weather.

Soil scientists may also specialize in one particular aspect of the work. For example, they may work as a *soil mapper* or *soil surveyor*. These specialists study soil structure, origins, and capabilities through field observations, laboratory examinations, and controlled experimentation. Their investigations are aimed at determining the most suitable uses for a particular soil.

Soil fertility experts develop practices that will increase or maintain crop size. They must consider both the type of soil and the

Soils on the Web

Visit the following Web sites to learn more about soil science and conservation:

Dig It: The Secrets of Soil
http://forces.si.edu/soils

The Dirt on Soil
http://school.discoveryeducation.com/schooladventures/soil/field_guide.html

S.K. Worm Answers Your Questions About Soil and Stuff!
http://www.nrcs.usda.gov/feature/education/squirm/skworm.html

Soil-net.com
http://www.soil-net.com

crop planted in their analysis. Various soils react differently when exposed to fertilizers, soil additives, crop rotation, and other farming techniques.

All soil scientists work in the laboratory. They examine soil samples under the microscope to determine bacterial and plant-food components. They also write reports based on their field notes and analyses done within the lab.

Soil science is part of the science of agronomy, which encompasses crop science. Soil and crop scientists work together in agricultural experiment stations during all seasons, doing research on crop production, soil fertility, and various kinds of soil management.

Some soil and crop scientists travel to remote sections of the world in search of plants and grasses that may thrive in this country and contribute to our food supply, pasture land, or soil replenishing efforts. Some scientists go overseas to advise farmers in other countries on how to treat their soils. Those with advanced degrees can teach college agriculture courses and conduct research projects.

REQUIREMENTS

High School

If you're interested in pursuing a career in agronomy, you should take college preparatory courses covering subjects such as math, science, English, and public speaking. Science courses, such as earth science, biology, and chemistry, are particularly important. Since much of your future work will involve calculations, you should take four years of high school math. You can learn a lot about farming methods and conditions by taking agriculture classes if your high school offers them. Computer science courses are also a good choice to familiarize yourself with this technology. You should also take English and speech courses, since soil scientists must write reports and make presentations about their findings.

Postsecondary Training

A bachelor's degree in agriculture or soil science is the minimum educational requirement to become a soil scientist. Typical courses include physics, geology, bacteriology, botany, chemistry, soil and plant morphology, soil fertility, soil classification, and soil genesis.

Research and teaching positions usually require higher levels of education. Most colleges of agriculture also offer master's and doctoral degrees. In addition to studying agriculture or soil science, students can specialize in biology, chemistry, physics, or engineering.

Certification or Licensing

Though not required, many soil scientists may seek certification to enhance their careers. The American Society of Agronomy and the Soil Science Society of America offer certification in the following areas: crop advisory, agronomy, and soil science/classification. In order to be accepted into a program, applicants must meet certain levels of education and experience.

The U.S. Department of Labor (DOL) reports that some states require soil scientists to be licensed. Typical licensing requirements include having a "bachelor's degree with a certain number of credit hours in soil science, a certain number of years working under a licensed scientist, and passage of an examination."

Other Requirements

Soil scientists must be able to work effectively both on their own and with others on projects, either outdoors or in the lab. Technology is increasingly used in this profession; an understanding of word processing, the Internet, multimedia software, databases, and even computer programming can be useful. Soil scientists spend many hours outdoors in all kinds of weather, so they must be able to endure sometimes difficult and uncomfortable physical conditions. They must be detail oriented to do accurate research, and they should enjoy solving puzzles—figuring out, for example, why a crop isn't flourishing and what fertilizers should be used.

EXPLORING

The National FFA Organization can introduce you to the concerns of farmers and researchers. Joining a 4-H club can also give you valuable experience in agriculture. Contact the local branch of these organizations, your county's soil conservation department, or other government agencies to learn about regional projects. If you live in an agricultural community, you may be able to find opportunities for part-time or summer work on a farm or ranch.

EMPLOYERS

Approximately 13,900 soil and plant scientists are employed in the United States. Most soil scientists work for state or federal departments of agriculture; others work for the U.S. Geological Survey. However, they may also work for other public employers, such as land appraisal boards, land-grant colleges and universities, and conservation departments. Soil scientists who work overseas may be employed by the U.S. Agency for International Development.

Soil scientists are needed in private industries as well, such as agricultural service companies, banks, insurance and real estate firms, food products companies, wholesale distributors, and environmental and engineering consulting groups. Private firms may hire soil scientists for sales or research positions.

STARTING OUT

In the public sector, college graduates can apply directly to the Natural Resources Conservation Service of the Department of Agriculture, the Department of the Interior, the Environmental Protection Agency, or other state government agencies for beginning positions. University career services offices generally have listings for these openings as well as opportunities available in private industry.

ADVANCEMENT

Salary increases are the most common form of advancement for soil scientists. The nature of the job may not change appreciably even after many years of service. Higher administrative and supervisory positions are few in comparison with the number of jobs that must be done in the field.

Opportunities for advancement will be higher for those with advanced degrees. For soil scientists engaged in teaching, advancement may translate into a higher academic rank with more responsibility. In private business firms, soil scientists have opportunities to advance into positions such as department head or research director. Supervisory and manager positions are also available in state agencies such as road or conservation departments.

EARNINGS

According to the DOL, median earnings in 2010 for soil and plant scientists were $57,340. The lowest paid 10 percent earned less than $34,420; the middle 50 percent earned between $44,390 and $74,630; and the highest paid 10 percent made more than $101,740.

Federal mean salaries for soil scientists were higher; in 2009, they made $78,250 a year. Government earnings depend in large part on levels of experience and education. Those with doctorates and a great deal of experience may qualify for higher government positions, with salaries ranging from $80,000 to $120,000. Other than short-term research projects, most jobs offer health and retirement benefits in addition to an annual salary.

WORK ENVIRONMENT

Most soil scientists work 40 hours a week. Their job is varied, ranging from fieldwork collecting samples, to labwork analyzing their findings. Some jobs may involve travel, even to foreign countries. Other positions may include teaching or supervisory responsibilities for field training programs.

OUTLOOK

The *Occupational Outlook Handbook* reports that employment within the field of soil science is expected to grow faster than the average for all occupations through 2018. Soil scientists will be needed to help create more food for our growing population, develop plans to fight erosion and other types of soil degradation, and help developers comply with environmental regulations.

The career of soil scientist is affected by the government's involvement in farming studies; as a result, budget cuts at the federal and (especially) state levels may limit funding for this type of job. However, private businesses will continue to demand soil scientists for research and sales positions. Companies dealing with seed, fertilizers, or farm equipment are examples of private employers that hire soil scientists.

Technological advances in equipment and methods of conservation will allow scientists to better protect the environment, as well as improve farm production. Scientists' ability to evaluate soils and plants will improve with more precise research methods. Combine-mounted yield monitors will produce data as the farmer crosses the field, and satellites will provide more detailed field information. With computer images, scientists will also be able to examine plant roots more carefully.

A continued challenge facing future soil scientists will be convincing farmers to change their current methods of tilling and chemical treatment in favor of environmentally safer methods. They must encourage farmers to balance increased agricultural output with the protection of our limited natural resources.

FOR MORE INFORMATION

For information on careers in geology, contact the following organizations:
American Geological Institute
4220 King Street
Alexandria, VA 22302-1502

Tel: 703-379-2480
http://www.agiweb.org

Geological Society of America
PO Box 9140
Boulder, CO 80301-9140
Tel: 888-443-4472
E-mail: gsaservice@geosociety.org
http://www.geosociety.org

The ASA has information on careers, certification, and college chapters. For details, contact
American Society of Agronomy (ASA)
5585 Guilford Road
Madison, WI 53711-5801
Tel: 608-273-8080
http://www.agronomy.org

Contact the NRCS for information on government soil conservation careers. Its Web site has information on volunteer opportunities.
Natural Resources Conservation Service (NRCS)
U.S. Department of Agriculture
1400 Independence Avenue, SW
Washington, DC 20250-0002
http://www.nrcs.usda.gov

For information on seminars, issues affecting soil scientists, and educational institutions offering soil science programs, contact
National Society of Consulting Soil Scientists
PO Box 1219
Sandpoint, ID 83864-0860
Tel: 800-535-7148
http://www.nscss.org

For information on soil conservation, college student chapters, and publications, contact
Soil and Water Conservation Society
945 SW Ankeny Road
Ankeny, IA 50023-9723
Tel: 515-289-2331
http://www.swcs.org

For information on certification and the career brochure Soils Sustain Life, *contact*
Soil Science Society of America
5585 Guilford Road
Madison, WI 53711-5801
Tel: 608-273-8080
http://www.soils.org

Surveying and Mapping Technicians

OVERVIEW

Surveying and mapping technicians help determine, describe, and record geographic areas or features. They are usually the leading assistant to the professional surveyor, civil engineer, and mapmaker (See "Surveyors"). They operate modern surveying and mapping instruments and may participate in other operations. Technicians must have a basic knowledge of the current practices and legal implications of surveys to establish and record property size, shape, topography, and boundaries. They often supervise other assistants during routine surveying conducted within the bounds established by a professional surveyor. There are approximately 77,000 surveying and mapping technicians working in the United States.

HISTORY

From ancient times, people have needed to define their property boundaries. Marking established areas of individual or group ownership was a basis for the development of early civilizations. Landholding became important in ancient Egypt, and with the development of hieroglyphics, people were able to keep a record of their holdings. Eventually, nations found it necessary not only to mark property boundaries but also to record principal routes of commerce and transportation. For example, records of the Babylonians tell of their canals and irrigation ditches. The Romans surveyed and mapped their empire's principal roads. In the early days of colonial exploration, surveyors and their technical helpers were among the first and most-needed workers. They established new land ownership by surveying and filing claims. Since then, precise and accurate geographical measurements have been needed to determine the location of a highway, the site of a building, the right-of-way for drainage ditches, telephone, and power lines, and for the charting of unexplored land, bodies of water, and underground mines.

Early surveying processes required at least two people. A technical scientist served as the leader, or professional surveyor. This scientist was assisted by helpers to make measurements with chains, tapes, and wheel rotations, where each rotation accounted for a known length of distance. The helpers held rods marked for location purposes and placed other markers to define important points.

As measuring instruments have become more complex, the speed, scope, and accuracy of surveying have improved. Developments in surveying and mapping technology have made great changes in the planning and construction of highway systems and structures of all kinds, as well as collecting various types of information for industry and government agencies. For roadway route selection and design, for example, technicians increasingly use photogrammetry to prepare digital or graphic maps. According to the U.S. Department of Labor (DOL), data for these maps is also gathered "using information provided by geodetic surveys and remote sensing systems including aerial cameras, satellites, light-imaging detection and ranging, or other technologies." Route data obtained by photogrammetry may then be processed through computers to calculate land acquisition, grading, and construction costs. Photogrammetry is faster and far more accurate than former methods. In addition, new electronic distance-measuring devices have brought surveying to a higher level of precision. Technicians can measure distance more quickly, accurately, and economically than was possible with tapes, rods, and chains.

In addition to photogrammetry, the use of computers in data processing has extended surveying and mapping careers past the earth's surface. Technicians now help to make detailed maps of ocean floors and the moon. Every rocket fired from the Kennedy Space Center is tracked electronically to determine if it is on course through the use of maps made by surveyors. The technological complexity of such undertakings allows surveyors to delegate more tasks than ever to technicians.

THE JOB

As essential assistants to civil engineers, surveyors, and mapmakers, surveying and mapping technicians are usually the first to be involved in any job that requires precise plotting. This includes highways, airports, housing developments, mines, dams, bridges, and buildings of all kinds.

The surveying and mapping technician is a key worker in field parties and major surveying projects and is often assigned the position of *chief instrument worker* under the surveyor's supervision. Technicians use a variety of surveying instruments, including the theodolite, transit, level, and other electronic equipment, to measure distances or locate a position. Technicians may be *rod workers*, using level rods or range poles to make elevation and distance measurements. They may also be *chain workers*, measuring shorter distances using a surveying chain or a metal tape. During the survey, it is important to accurately record all readings and keep orderly field notes to check for accuracy.

Surveying and mapping technicians may specialize if they join a firm that focuses on one or more particular types of surveying. In a firm that specializes in land surveying, technicians are highly skilled in technical measuring and tasks related to establishing township, property, and other tract-of-land boundary lines. They help the professional surveyor with maps, notes, and title deeds. They help survey the land, check the accuracy of existing records, and prepare legal documents such as deeds and leases.

Similarly, technicians who work for highway, pipeline, railway, or power line surveying firms help to establish grades, lines, and other points of reference for construction projects. This survey information provides the exact locations for engineering design and construction work.

Technicians who work for geodetic surveyors help take measurements of large masses of land, sea, or space. These measurements must take into account the curvature of the earth and its geophysical characteristics. Their findings set major points of reference for smaller land surveys, determining national boundaries, and preparing maps.

Technicians may also specialize in hydrographic surveying, measuring harbors, rivers, and other bodies of water. These surveys are needed to design navigation systems, prepare nautical maps and charts, establish property boundaries, and plan for breakwaters, levees, dams, locks, piers, and bridges.

Mining surveying technicians are usually on the geological staffs of either mining companies or exploration companies. In recent years, costly new surveying instruments have changed the way they do their jobs. Using highly technical machinery, technicians can map underground geology, take samples, locate diamond drill holes, log drill cores, and map geological data derived from boreholes. They also map data on mine plans and diagrams and help the geologist determine ore reserves. In the search for new mines, technicians operate delicate instruments to obtain data on variations in the earth's magnetic field, its conductivity, and gravity. They use their data to map the boundaries of areas for potential further exploration.

Surveying and mapping technicians may find topographical surveys to be interesting and challenging work. These surveys determine the contours of the land and indicate such features as mountains, lakes, rivers, forests, roads, farms, buildings, and other distinguishable landmarks. In topographical surveying, technicians help take aerial or land photographs with photogrammetric equipment installed in an airplane or ground station that can take pictures of large areas. This method is widely used to measure farmland planted with certain crops and to verify crop average allotments under government production planning quotas.

A large number of survey technicians are employed in construction work. Technicians are needed from start to finish on any job. They check the construction of a structure for size, height, depth, level, and form specifications. They also use measurements to locate the critical construction points as specified by design plans, such as corners of buildings, foundation points, center points for columns, walls, and other features, floor or ceiling levels, and other features that require precise measurements and location.

Technological advances such as the global positioning system (GPS) and geographic information systems (GIS) have revolutionized surveying and mapping work. Using these systems, surveying teams can track points on the earth with radio signals transmitted from satellites and store this information in computer databases.

REQUIREMENTS

High School

If you are interested in becoming a surveying and mapping technician, take mathematics courses, such as algebra, geometry, and trigonometry, as well as mechanical drawing in high school. Physics, chemistry, and biology are other valuable classes that will help you gain laboratory experience. Reading, writing, and comprehension skills as well as knowledge of computers are also vital in surveying and mapping, so English and computer science courses are also highly recommended.

Postsecondary Training

Though not required to enter the field, graduates of accredited post-secondary training programs for surveying, photogrammetry, and mapping are in the best position to become surveying and mapping technicians. Postsecondary training is available from institutional programs and correspondence schools. These demanding technical programs generally last two years with a possible field study in the summer. First-year courses include English, composition, computer-aided drafting, applied mathematics, surveying and measurements, construction materials and methods, applied physics, statistics, and computer applications. Second-year courses cover subjects such as technical physics, advanced surveying, photogrammetry and mapping, soils and foundations, technical reporting, legal issues, and transportation and environmental engineering. Contact the American Congress on Surveying and Mapping (ACSM) for a list of accredited programs (see the end of this article for contact information).

With additional experience and study, technicians can specialize in geodesy, topography, hydrography, or photogrammetry. Many graduates of two-year programs later pursue a bachelor's degree in surveying, engineering, or geomatics.

Certification or Licensing

Unlike professional land surveyors, there are no certification or licensing requirements for becoming a surveying and mapping technician. However, technicians who seek government employment must pass a civil service examination.

Many employers prefer certified technicians for promotions into higher positions with more responsibility. The National Society of Professional Surveyors, a member organization of the ACSM, offers the voluntary survey technician certification at four levels. With each level, the technician must have more experience and pass progressively challenging examinations. If the technician hopes one day to work as a surveyor, he or she must be specially certified to work in his or her state.

The American Society for Photogrammetry and Remote Sensing offers voluntary certification for technicians who specialize in photogrammetry, remote sensing, and GIS.

Technicians who use GIS technology in their work can receive voluntary certification from the GIS Certification Institute. Applicants must have a baccalaureate degree in any field, complete coursework and other documented education in GIS and geospatial data technologies, have work experience in a GIS-related position, and participate in conferences or GIS-related events. Applicants who meet all certification requirements may use the designation certified GIS professional. Certification must be renewed every five years.

Other Requirements

To be a successful surveying and mapping technician, you must be patient, orderly, systematic, accurate, and objective in your work. You must be willing to work cooperatively and have the ability to think and plan ahead. Because of the increasing technical nature of their work, you must have computer skills to be able to use highly complex equipment such as GPS and GIS technology.

EXPLORING

One of the best opportunities for experience is to work part time or during your summer vacation for a construction firm or a company involved in survey work. Even if the job does not involve direct contact with survey crews, you may be able to observe their work and converse with them to discover more about their daily activities. Another possibility is to work for a government agency overseeing land use. The Bureau of Land Management, for example, has employment opportunities for students who qualify, as well as many volunteer positions. The Forest Service also offers temporary positions for students.

EMPLOYERS

There are approximately 77,000 surveying and mapping technicians working in the United States. About 70 percent of technicians find work with engineering or architectural service firms. The federal government also employs a number of technicians to work for the U.S. Geological Survey, the Bureau of Land Management, the National Oceanic and Atmospheric Administration, the National Geospatial-Intelligence Agency, and the Forest Service. State and local governments also hire surveying and mapping technicians to work for highway departments and urban planning agencies. Construction firms and oil, gas, and mining companies also employ technicians.

STARTING OUT

If you plan on entering surveying straight from high school, you may first work as an apprentice. Through on-the-job training and some classroom work, apprentices build up their skills and knowledge of the trade to eventually become surveying and mapping technicians.

If you plan to attend a technical institute or four-year college, contact your school's career services office for help in arranging examinations or interviews. Employers of surveying technicians often send recruiters to schools before graduation and arrange to employ promising graduates. Some community or technical colleges have work-study programs that provide cooperative part-time or summer work for pay. Employers involved with these programs often hire students full time after graduation.

Finally, many cities have employment agencies that specialize in placing technical workers in positions in surveying, mapping, construction, mining, and related fields. Check your local newspaper or telephone book, or surf the Web, to see if your town offers these services.

ADVANCEMENT

Possibilities for advancement are linked to levels of formal education and experience. As technicians gain experience and technical knowledge, they can advance to positions of greater responsibility and eventually work as chief surveyor. To advance into this position, technicians will most likely need a two- or four-year degree in surveying and many years of experience. Also, all 50 states require surveyors to be licensed, requiring varying amounts of experience, education, and examinations.

Regardless of the level of advancement, all surveying and mapping technicians must continue studying to keep up with the technological developments in their field. Technological advances in computers, lasers, and microcomputers will continue to change job requirements. Studying to keep up with changes combined with progressive experience gained on the job will increase the technician's opportunity for advancement.

EARNINGS

According to the DOL, the 2010 median hourly wage for all surveying and mapping technicians, regardless of the industry, was $18.22 (amounting to $37,900 for full-time work). The lowest paid 10 percent earned less than $11.28 ($23,450 for full-time work), and the highest paid 10 percent earned more than $29.27 an hour (or $60,870 annually for full-time work). Technicians working in the public sector for federal, state, and local governments generally earn more per hour than those working in the private sector for engineering and architectural services. In 2010, surveying and mapping technicians working for the federal government made a mean annual salary of $47,350. Those who worked in the oil and gas extraction industries earned $56,360.

Benefits for salaried surveying and mapping technicians depend on the employer; however, they usually include such items as health insurance, retirement or 401(k) plans, and paid vacation days. Self-employed workers must provide their own benefits.

WORK ENVIRONMENT

Surveying and mapping technicians usually work about 40 hours a week except when overtime is necessary. The peak work period for many kinds of surveying work is during the summer months when weather conditions are most favorable. However, surveying crews are exposed to all types of weather conditions.

Some survey projects involve certain hazards depending upon the region and the climate as well as local plant and animal life. Field survey crews may encounter snakes and poison ivy. They are subject to heat exhaustion, sunburn, and frostbite. Some projects, particularly those being conducted near construction projects or busy highways, impose dangers of injury from cars and flying debris. Unless survey technicians are employed for office assignments, their work location changes from survey to survey. Some assignments may require technicians to be away from home for varying periods of time.

While on the job, technicians who supervise other workers must take special care to observe good safety practices. Construction and mining workplaces usually require hard hats, special clothing, and protective shoes.

OUTLOOK

Employment for surveying and mapping technicians is expected to grow about as fast as the average for all occupations through 2018, according to the DOL. New technologies—such as GPS, GIS, and remote sensing—have allowed surveying professionals to gather an increasing amount of geographic information that can be used, according to the DOL, to "create maps and information used in emergency planning, security, marketing, urban planning, natural resource exploration, construction, and other applications."

Another factor that may increase the demand for surveying services, and therefore surveying technicians, is growth in urban and suburban areas. New streets, homes, shopping centers, schools, and gas and water lines will require property and boundary line surveys. Other factors are the continuing state and federal highway improvement programs and the increasing number of urban redevelopment programs. The expansion of industrial and business firms and the relocation of some firms in large undeveloped areas are also expected to create a need for surveying services.

The need to replace workers who have either retired or transferred to other occupations will also provide opportunities. In general, technicians with more education and skill training will have more job options.

FOR MORE INFORMATION

For more information on accredited surveying programs, contact
Accreditation Board for Engineering and Technology Inc.
111 Market Place, Suite 1050
Baltimore, MD 21202-7116
Tel: 410-347-7700
E-mail: accreditation@abet.org
http://www.abet.org

For information on careers, scholarships, certification, and educational programs, contact
American Congress on Surveying and Mapping
6 Montgomery Village Avenue, Suite 403
Gaithersburg, MD 20879-3557
Tel: 240-632-9716
http://www.acsm.net

For information on careers and certification, contact
American Society for Photogrammetry and Remote Sensing
5410 Grosvenor Lane, Suite 210
Bethesda, MD 20814-2160
Tel: 301-493-0290
E-mail: asprs@asprs.org
http://www.asprs.org

Visit the society's Web site to read Cartography and GIS.
Cartography and Geographic Information Society
6 Montgomery Village Avenue, Suite 403
Gaithersburg, MD 20879-3557
Tel: 240-632-9716
http://www.cartogis.org

For more information on certification, contact
GIS Certification Institute
701 Lee Street, Suite 680
Des Plaines, IL 60016-4508
Tel: 847-824-7768
E-mail: info@gisci.org
http://www.gisci.org

For more information on geographic information systems (GIS),
visit the following Web site:
GIS.com
http://www.gis.com

For information on certification, contact
National Society of Professional Surveyors
6 Montgomery Village Avenue, Suite 403
Gaithersburg, MD 20879-3557
Tel: 240-632-9716
http://www.nspsmo.org

Surveyors

OVERVIEW

Surveyors mark exact measurements and locations of elevations, points, lines, and contours on or near the earth's surface. They measure distances between points to determine property boundaries and to provide data for mapmaking, construction projects, and other engineering purposes. In addition to working outdoors, surveyors also spend time in offices studying data and writing reports and in courthouses conducting research. There are approximately 147,000 surveyors, cartographers, photogrammetrists, and surveying technicians employed in the United States. Of those, about 57,600 are surveyors and about 12,300 are cartographers and photogrammetrists.

HISTORY

As the United States expanded from the Atlantic Ocean to the Pacific, people moved over the mountains and plains into the uncharted regions of the West. They found it necessary to chart their routes and to mark property lines and borderlines by surveying and filing claims.

The need for accurate geographical measurements and precise records of those measurements has increased over the years. Surveying measurements are needed to determine the location of a trail, highway, or road; the site of a log cabin, frame house, or skyscraper; the right-of-way for water pipes, drainage ditches, and telephone lines; and for the charting of unexplored regions, bodies of water, land, and underground mines.

As a result, the demand for professional surveyors has grown and become more complex. New computerized systems are now used

Surveyors must have the ability to visualize and understand objects in two and three dimensions. *(Ron Nichols, Natural Resources Conservation Service)*

to map, store, and retrieve geographical data more accurately and efficiently. This new technology has not only improved the process of surveying but extended its reach as well. Surveyors can now make detailed maps of ocean floors and the moon's surface.

THE JOB

It is the surveyor's responsibility to make necessary measurements through an accurate and detailed survey of the area and prepare maps, plots, and reports. The surveyor usually works with a field party consisting of several people. Instrument assistants, called *surveying and mapping technicians*, handle a variety of surveying instruments including the theodolite, transit, steel tapes, level, surveyor's chain, rod, and 3-D laser scanners, lasers, and other electronic equipment. (See "Surveying and Mapping Technicians"). They also use the global positioning system (GPS) to take measurements. GPS is a group of satellites above the earth that communicate with receivers on the ground to provide extremely accurate information about the location of the area being measured. In the course of the survey, it is important that all readings be recorded accurately and field notes maintained so that the survey can be checked for accuracy. The *party chief* is a surveyor or surveying and mapping technician who supervises the daily activities of the survey team.

Surveyors may specialize in one or more particular types of surveying.

Construction surveyors make surveys for construction projects, such as highways, bridges, airstrips, shopping centers, and housing developments. They establish grades, lines, and other points of reference for construction projects. This survey information is essential to the work of the numerous engineers and the construction crews who build these projects.

Mine surveyors make surface and underground surveys, preparing maps of mines and mining operations. Such maps are helpful in examining underground passages within the levels of a mine and assessing the volume and location of raw material available.

Geophysical prospecting surveyors locate and mark sites considered likely to contain petroleum deposits. *Oil-well directional surveyors* use sonic, electronic, and nuclear measuring instruments to gauge the presence and amount of oil- and gas-bearing reservoirs. *Pipeline surveyors* determine rights-of-way for oil construction projects, providing information essential to the preparation for and laying of the lines.

Land surveyors establish township, property, and other tract-of-land boundary lines. Using maps, notes, or actual land title deeds, they survey the land, checking for the accuracy of existing records. This information is used to prepare legal documents such as deeds and leases. Land surveyors are also known as *boundary*, or *cadastral, surveyors*. *Land surveying managers* coordinate the work of surveyors, their parties, and legal, engineering, architectural, and other staff involved in a project. In addition, these managers develop policy, prepare budgets, certify work upon completion, and handle numerous other administrative duties.

Geodetic surveyors, also known as *geodesists*, use satellite observations and other high-accuracy techniques to measure large masses of land, sea, and space that must take into account the curvature of the earth and its geophysical characteristics. Their work is helpful in establishing points of reference for smaller land surveys, determining national boundaries, and preparing maps. *Geodetic computers* calculate latitude, longitude, angles, areas, and other information needed for mapmaking. They work from field notes made by an engineering survey party and also use reference tables and a calculating machine or computer.

Marine surveyors, also known as *hydrographic surveyors*, measure harbors, rivers, and other bodies of water. They determine the depth of the water through measuring sound waves in relation to nearby landmasses. Their work is essential for planning and constructing navigation projects, such as breakwaters, dams, piers, marinas, and bridges, and for preparing nautical charts and maps.

Photogrammetric engineers, also known as *photogrammetrists*, determine the contour of an area to show elevations and depressions and indicate such features as mountains, lakes, rivers, forests, roads, farms, buildings, and other landmarks. Aerial, land, and water photographs are taken with special equipment able to capture images of very large areas. From these pictures, accurate measurements of the terrain and surface features can be made. These surveys are helpful in construction projects and in the preparation of topographical maps. Photogrammetry is particularly helpful in charting areas that are inaccessible or to which travel is difficult.

Forensic surveyors serve as expert witnesses in legal proceedings that involve industrial, automobile, or other types of accidents. They gather, analyze, and map data that is used as evidence at a trial, hearing, or lawsuit. These professionals must have extensive experience in the field and be strong communicators in order to explain technical information to people who do not have a background in surveying.

REQUIREMENTS

High School

Does this work interest you? If so, you should prepare for it by taking plenty of math and science courses in high school. Take algebra, geometry, and trigonometry to become comfortable making different calculations. Earth science, chemistry, and physics classes will also be helpful. Geography will help you learn about different locations, their characteristics, and cartography. Benefits from taking mechanical drawing and other drafting classes include an increased ability to visualize abstractions, exposure to detailed work, and an understanding of perspectives. Taking computer science classes will prepare you for working with technical surveying equipment.

Postsecondary Training

You will need a bachelor's degree in surveying to gain employment in this field. Photogrammetrists typically have a bachelor's degree in cartography, geography, surveying, computer science, engineering, forestry, or a physical science.

Certification or Licensing

The American Congress on Surveying and Mapping (ACSM) has partnered with the Federal Emergency Management Agency to create a certification program for floodplain surveyors. Contact the ACSM for details on the program. The ACSM has also partnered with the Bureau of Land Management to create the certified federal surveyors program. Contact the ACSM for more information.

The American Society for Photogrammetry and Remote Sensing offers voluntary certification for surveyors who specialize in photogrammetry and GIS. Certification is also provided by the GIS Certification Institute.

All 50 states require that surveyors making property and boundary surveys be licensed or registered. The requirements for licensure vary, but most require a degree in surveying or a related field, a certain number of years of experience, and passing a series of written examinations given by the National Council of Examiners for Engineering and Surveying. Information on specific requirements can be obtained by contacting the licensure department of the state in which you plan to work. If you are seeking employment in the federal government, you must take a civil service examination and meet the educational, experience, and other specified requirements for the position.

Other Requirements

The ability to work with numbers and perform mathematical computations accurately and quickly is very important. Other helpful qualities are the ability to visualize and understand objects in two and three dimensions (spatial relationships) and the ability to discriminate between and compare shapes, sizes, lines, shadings, and other forms (form perception).

Surveyors walk a great deal and carry equipment over all types of terrain so endurance and coordination are important physical assets. In addition, surveyors direct and supervise the work of their team, so you should be good at working with other people and demonstrate leadership abilities.

EXPLORING

While you are in high school, begin to familiarize yourself with terms, projects, and tools used in this profession by reading books and magazines on the topic. One magazine that is available online is *Professional Surveyor Magazine* at http://www.profsurv.com. One of the best opportunities for experience is a summer job with a construction outfit, a mining company, or a company that requires survey work. Even if the job does not involve direct contact with survey crews, it will offer an opportunity to observe surveyors and talk with them about their work.

Some colleges have work-study programs that offer on-the-job experience. These opportunities, like summer or part-time jobs, provide helpful contacts in the field that may lead to future full-time employment. If your college does not offer a work-study program and you can't find a paying summer job, consider volunteering at an appropriate government agency. The U.S. Geological Survey and the Bureau of Land Management usually have volunteer opportunities in select areas.

EMPLOYERS

Approximately 57,600 surveyors are employed in the United States. About 70 percent of surveying workers in the United States are employed by engineering, architectural, and surveying firms. Federal, state, and local government agencies are the next largest employers of surveying workers. Federal agencies that employ a large number of surveyors include the U.S. Geological Survey, the Bureau of Land Management, the National Oceanic and Atmospheric Administration, the U.S. Forest Service, and the Army Corps of Engineers. The majority of the remaining surveyors work for construction firms, highway departments, oil and gas extraction companies, public utilities, and urban planning and redevelopment agencies. Only a small number of surveyors are self-employed.

STARTING OUT

Apprentices with a high school education can enter the field as equipment operators or surveying assistants. Those who have postsecondary education can enter the field more easily, beginning as surveying and mapping technicians.

College graduates can learn about job openings through their schools' career services offices or through potential employers that may visit their campus. Many cities have employment agencies that specialize in seeking out workers for positions in surveying and related fields. Check your local newspaper or telephone book to see if such recruiting firms exist in your area.

ADVANCEMENT

With experience, workers advance through the leadership ranks within a surveying team. Workers begin as assistants and then can move into positions such as senior technician, party chief, and, finally, licensed surveyor. Because surveying work is closely related to other fields, surveyors can move into electrical, mechanical, or chemical engineering or specialize in drafting.

EARNINGS

Surveyors earned a median annual salary of $54,880 in 2010, according to the U.S. Department of Labor (DOL). The middle 50 percent earned between $40,260 and $72,360 a year. The lowest paid 10 percent earned less than $30,800, and the highest paid 10 percent earned more than $89,930 a year. In general, the federal government paid the highest average wages to its surveyors, $82,230 a year in 2010.

Most positions with the federal, state, and local governments and with private firms provide life and medical insurance, pension, vacation, and holiday benefits.

WORK ENVIRONMENT

Surveyors work 40-hour weeks except when overtime is necessary to meet a project deadline. The peak work period is during the summer months when weather conditions are most favorable. However, it is not uncommon for the surveyor to be exposed to adverse weather conditions.

Some survey projects may involve hazardous conditions, depending on the region and climate as well as the plant and animal life. Survey crews may encounter snakes, poison ivy, and other hazardous plant and animal life, and may suffer heat exhaustion, sunburn, and frostbite while in the field. Survey projects, particularly those near construction projects or busy highways, may impose dangers of injury from heavy traffic, flying objects, and other accidental hazards. Unless the surveyor is employed only for office assignments, the work location most likely will change from survey to survey. Some assignments may require the surveyor to be away from home for periods of time.

OUTLOOK

The DOL predicts that the employment of surveyors will grow faster than the average for all occupations through 2018. The outlook is best for surveyors who have college degrees, advanced field experience, and knowledge of global positioning system and geographic information systems technology. Growth in urban and suburban areas (with the need for new streets, homes, shopping centers, schools, gas and water lines) will provide employment opportunities. State and federal highway improvement programs and local urban redevelopment programs also will provide jobs for surveyors. The expansion of industrial and business firms and the relocation of some firms to large undeveloped tracts will also create job openings. However, construction projects are closely tied to the state of the economy, so employment may fluctuate from year to year.

FOR MORE INFORMATION

For information on geodetic surveying, contact
American Association for Geodetic Surveying
http://www.aagsmo.org

For information on state affiliates and colleges and universities offering land surveying programs, contact
American Congress on Surveying and Mapping
6 Montgomery Village Avenue, Suite 403
Gaithersburg, MD 20879-3557
Tel: 240-632-9716
http://www.acsm.net

For information on volunteer and employment opportunities with the federal government, contact the following organizations:
Bureau of Land Management
http://www.blm.gov

National Oceanic and Atmospheric Administration
http://www.noaa.gov

U.S. Army Corps of Engineers
http://www.usace.army.mil

U.S. Environmental Protection Agency
http://water.epa.gov/drink/index.cfm

U.S. Forest Service
http://www.fs.fed.us

U.S. Geological Survey
http://www.usgs.gov

For information on careers, contact
American Society for Photogrammetry and Remote Sensing
5410 Grosvenor Lane, Suite 210
Bethesda, MD 20814-2160
Tel: 301-493-0290
E-mail: asprs@asprs.org
http://www.asprs.org

Visit the society's Web site to read Cartography and GIS.
Cartography and Geographic Information Society
6 Montgomery Village Avenue, Suite 403
Gaithersburg, MD 20879-3557
Tel: 240-632-9716
http://www.cartogis.org

For more information on certification, contact
GIS Certification Institute
701 Lee Street, Suite 680
Des Plaines, IL 60016-4508
Tel: 847-824-7768
E-mail: info@gisci.org
http://www.gisci.org

For career information, contact
National Society of Professional Surveyors
6 Montgomery Village Avenue, Suite 403
Gaithersburg, MD 20879-3557
Tel: 240-632-9716
http://www.nspsmo.org

Index

Entries and page numbers in **bold** indicate
major treatment of a topic.